USING CONVERSATION ANALYSIS

for *BUSINESS and* MANAGEMENT STUDENTS

Sara Miller McCune founded SAGE Publishing in 1965 to support the dissemination of usable knowledge and educate a global community. SAGE publishes more than 1000 journals and over 800 new books each year, spanning a wide range of subject areas. Our growing selection of library products includes archives, data, case studies and video. SAGE remains majority owned by our founder and after her lifetime will become owned by a charitable trust that secures the company's continued independence.

Los Angeles | London | New Delhi | Singapore | Washington DC | Melbourne

USING CONVERSATION ANALYSIS

for BUSINESS *and* MANAGEMENT STUDENTS

DAVID GREATBATCH & TIMOTHY CLARK

Los Angeles | London | New Delhi
Singapore | Washington DC | Melbourne

Los Angeles | London | New Delhi
Singapore | Washington DC | Melbourne

SAGE Publications Ltd
1 Oliver's Yard
55 City Road
London EC1Y 1SP

SAGE Publications Inc.
2455 Teller Road
Thousand Oaks, California 91320

SAGE Publications India Pvt Ltd
B 1/I 1 Mohan Cooperative Industrial Area
Mathura Road
New Delhi 110 044

SAGE Publications Asia-Pacific Pte Ltd
3 Church Street
#10-04 Samsung Hub
Singapore 049483

Editor: Kirsty Smy
Assistant editor: Lyndsay Aitken
Production editor: Sarah Cooke
Copyeditor: William Buginsky
Proofreader: Tom Hickman
Indexer: Judith Lavender
Marketing manager: Alison Borg
Cover design: Francis Kenney
Typeset by: C&M Digitals (P) Ltd, Chennai, India
Printed in the UK

© David Greatbatch and Timothy Clark 2018

Editors' Introduction © Bill Lee, Mark N. K. Saunders and
Vadake K. Narayanan 2018
First published 2018

Library of Congress Control Number: 2017938806

British Library Cataloguing in Publication data

A catalogue record for this book is available from
the British Library

ISBN 978-1-47394-825-9
ISBN 978-1-47394-826-6 (pbk)

At SAGE we take sustainability seriously. Most of our products are printed in the UK using FSC papers and boards.
When we print overseas we ensure sustainable papers are used as measured by the PREPS grading system.
We undertake an annual audit to monitor our sustainability.

For Sallie and Penny
And our children
Emily and Olivia; Max and India

CONTENTS

EDITORS' INTRODUCTION TO THE *MASTERING BUSINESS RESEARCH METHODS* SERIES

Welcome to the *Mastering Business Research Methods* series. In recent years, there has been a great increase in the numbers of students reading masters level degrees across the business and management disciplines. A great number of these students have to prepare a dissertation towards the end of their degree programme in a time-frame of three to four months. For many students, this takes place after their taught modules have finished and is expected to be an independent piece of work. While each student is supported in their dissertation or research project by an academic super-visor, the student will need to find out more detailed information about the method that he or she intends to use. Before starting their dissertations or research projects these students have usually been provided with little more than an overview across a wide range of methods as preparation for this often daunting task. If you are one such student, you are not alone. As university professors with a deep interest in research methods, we have provided this series of books to help students like you. Each book provides detailed information about a particular method to support you in your dis-sertation. We understand both what is involved in masters level dissertations, and what help students need with regard to methods in order to excel when writing a dissertation. This series is the only one that is designed with the specific objective of helping masters level students to undertake and prepare their dissertations.

Each book in our series is designed to provide sufficient knowledge about either a method of data collection or a method of data analysis, and each book is intended to be read by the student when undertaking particular stages of the research pro-cess, such as data collection or analysis. Each book is written in a clear way by highly respected authors who have considerable experience of teaching and writing about research methods. To help students find their way around each book, we have utilized a standard format, with each book having been organized into six chapters:

- **Chapter 1** introduces the method, considers how the method emerged for what purposes, and provides an outline of the remainder of the book.
- **Chapter 2** addresses the underlying philosophical assumptions that inform the uses of particular methods.
- **Chapter 3** discusses the components of the relevant method.
- **Chapter 4** considers the way in which the different components may be organized to use the method.
- **Chapter 5** provides examples of published studies that have used the method.
- **Chapter 6** concludes by reflecting on the strengths and weaknesses of that method.

We hope that reading your chosen books helps you in your dissertation.

Bill Lee, Mark NK Saunders and VK Narayanan

ABOUT THE SERIES EDITORS

Bill Lee, PhD, is Professor of Accounting and Head of the Accounting and Financial Management Division at the University of Sheffield, UK. He has a long-standing interest in research methods and practice, in addition to his research into accounting and accountability issues. Bill's research has been published widely, including in: *Accounting Forum*; *British Accounting Review*; *Critical Perspectives on Accounting*; *Management Accounting Research*; *Omega*; and *Work, Employment & Society*. His publications in the area of research methods and practice include the co-edited collections *The Real Life Guide to Accounting Research* and *Challenges and Controversies in Management Research*.

Mark NK Saunders, BA MSc PGCE PhD FCIPD, is Professor of Business Research Methods at Birmingham Business School, University of Birmingham, UK. His research interests are research methods, in particular methods for understanding intra organisational relationships; human resource aspects of the management of change, in particular trust within and between organizations; and small and medium-sized enterprises. Mark's research has been published in journals including *Journal of Small Business Management*, *Field Methods*, *Human Relations*, *Management Learning* and *Social Science and Medicine*. He has co-authored and co-edited a range of books including *Research Methods for Business Students* (currently in its sixth edition) and the *Handbook of Research Methods on Trust*.

VK Narayanan is the Associate Dean for Research, Director of the Center for Research Excellence, and the Deloitte Touché Stubbs Professor of Strategy and Entrepreneurship in Drexel University, Philadelphia, PA. His articles have appeared in leading professional journals such as *Academy of Management Journal*, *Academy of Management Review*, *Accounting Organizations and Society*, *Journal of Applied Psychology*, *Journal of Management*, *Journal of Management Studies*, *Management Information Systems Quarterly*, *R&D Management* and *Strategic Management*

Journal. Narayanan holds a bachelor's degree in mechanical engineering from the Indian Institute of Technology, Madras, a postgraduate degree in business administration from the Indian Institute of Management, Ahmedabad, and a Ph.D. in business from the Graduate School of Business at the University of Pittsburgh, Pennsylvania.

ABOUT THE AUTHORS

David Greatbatch is a Visiting Professor at Durham University Business School and has previously held positions at the Universities of Nottingham, Oxford, London and Warwick, and the Xerox Research Laboratory in Cambridge. He has undertaken studies using conversation analysis in a wide variety of contexts including, management consultancy, live corporate events, broadcast journalism, general practice and telemedicine. He has published articles in leading international journals such as *American Journal of Sociology*, *American Sociological Review*, *Language in Society*, *Human Relations*, *Leadership Quarterly*, *The Sociology of Health and Illness*, *Management Communication Quarterly*, *Interacting with Computers*, and *Law and Society Review*. He co-authored *Management Speak* (Routledge, 2005) with Timothy Clark.

Timothy Clark is Professor of Organisational Behaviour and Pro-Vice-Chancellor (Social Sciences & Health) at Durham University, UK. He has conducted a series of studies into different aspects of the activities of management consultants and management gurus. These projects have resulted in a number of publications in a range of journals as well as books, which include *Management Speak* (Routledge, 2005) with David Greatbatch. He is a past General Editor of *Journal of Management Studies* and past President of the British Academy of Management.

ACKNOWLEDGEMENTS

We are grateful for permission to reproduce the following copyright material:

Atkinson, J.M. and P, Drew, P. (1979) Order in Court: The Organisation of Verbal

Interaction in Judicial Settings. London: Macmillan. Extracts in Chapter 3 reprinted by permission of Springer Nature.

Greatbatch, D. (1992) 'On the management of disagreement between news interviewees'. In P. Drew and J.C. Heritage (eds) Talk at Work: Interaction in Institutional Settings. Cambridge: Cambridge University Press, pp. 268-301. Extracts in Box 3.1 reprinted with permission of Cambridge University Press.

Sacks, H., Schegloff, E.A. and Jefferson, G. (1974) 'A simplest systematics for the organization of turn taking for conversation', Language, 50: 696-735. Quotes in Chapter 3 republished with permission of the Linguistic Society of America; permission conveyed through Copyright Clearance Center, Inc.

Greatbatch, D. and Clark, T. (2003) 'Displaying group cohesiveness: humour and laughter in the public lectures of management gurus'. Human Relations, 56 (12): 1515-44. Extract in 'Case Study: Management Guru Lectures' in Chapter 4 reprinted by permission of SAGE Publications.

Larsson, M. and Lundholm, S.E. (2013) 'Talking work in a bank: A study of organizing properties of leadership in work interactions'. Human Relations, 66 (8): 1101-29. Extract in Box 5.1 reprinted by permission of SAGE Publications.

Huisman, M. (2001) 'Decision-making in meetings as talk in-interaction'. International Studies of Management & Organization, 31 (3): 69-90. Extract in Box 5.2 reprinted by permission of the publisher (Taylor & Francis Ltd, http://www.tandfonline.com).

Kangasharju, H., and Nikko, T. (2009) 'Emotions in organizations: Joint laughter in workplace meetings'. Journal of Business Communication, 46: 100-19. Extract in Box 5.3 reprinted by permission of SAGE Publications.

Oshima, S. (2014) 'Achieving consensus through professionalized head nods: The role of nodding in service encounters in Japan'. Journal of Business Communication, 51 (1): 31-57. Extract in Box 5.5 reprinted by permission of SAGE Publications.

Scheuer, J. (2014) 'Managing employees' talk about problems in work in performance appraisal interviews'. Discourse Studies. 16 (3): 407-429. Extract in Box 5.4 reprinted by permission of SAGE Publications.

1

INTRODUCTION

Conversation analysis (CA) is an approach to the study of everyday instances of human social interaction that is used in many areas of research, including sociology, psychology, various subfields of linguistics, communication studies, media studies, education, computer science as well as business and management research. CA is primarily concerned with studying talk-in-interaction, but it also considers the nonverbal aspects of social interaction such as gaze direction, gestures and body movement and how verbal and nonverbal features of interaction relate to one another. It involves detailed analysis of audio or video recordings of naturally occurring social interaction, focusing on observable interactional phenomena such as how people allocate turns at talk, how they introduce and change topics, how they handle disagreements, and how they repair problems in speaking, hearing or understanding. Although CA was initially largely focused on the study of casual conversations, it has subsequently been applied to social interaction in a wide range of organizational settings in the public, private and not-for-profit sectors. Despite its name, CA is a generic approach to the study of social interaction.

The relevance of CA to business and management research should be self-evident given that talk-in-interaction is a pervasive feature of the day-to-day operations in any organization and is central to the accomplishment of key business and management activities, such as strategizing, planning, selling, interviewing, chairing meetings, negotiating and presenting. If you have access to audio or video recordings of naturally occurring talk in organizational settings – collected by you, an organization or available on the web – then CA is an excellent choice for your research. It offers a rigorous and systematic approach to transcribing and analysing these data and provides fascinating and important insights into the tacit practices and knowledge that underpin the accomplishment of organizational activities, such as those mentioned above. You will also be able to draw upon a substantial body of research conducted over the last half-century that has applied the approach and findings of CA to talk in organizational settings, including a growing corpus of literature within the business and management field.

Our aim in this book is to provide you with the information and guidance you need to use CA successfully for data analysis in your own research. We will explain how CA emerged, its underlying philosophical assumptions, its methodology and the steps involved in the process of carrying out a CA study. We will also provide you with detailed examples of published CA studies in the field of business and management, including an example from our own research so that you are aware of its application and have examples from which you can draw for your own studies. Finally, we will conclude by reflecting on the overall strengths and limitations of CA, helping you to make a persuasive case for the methodology and the way that you have used it.

In the remainder of this chapter, we briefly explain the historical emergence of CA in sociology, its subsequent diffusion across a range of academic fields and its use within business and management research.

OVERVIEW OF CONVERSATION ANALYSIS

History of Conversation Analysis

CA emerged in the 1960s as part of the broader programme of research known as ethnomethodology, which was founded by the sociologist Harold Garfinkel (1917–2011). The aim of ethnomethodology is to document the commonsense knowledge and practices that people use to navigate their daily lives and tasks. In his early studies, Garfinkel (1963, 1967) examined the presuppositions about actions and motives that people rely on when involved in everyday activities such as deliberating on juries, talking to counsellors, playing the paper and pencil game tic-tac-toe (also known as noughts and crosses), requesting help from shop assistants and doing 'being a natural, normal female'. Garfinkel advocated treating everyday activities as 'anthropologically strange' in order to detect the underlying tacit expectancies 'that lend commonsense scenes their familiar, life-as-usual character' (Garfinkel, 1967: 37).

Drawing on ethnomethodology, another sociologist Harvey Sacks (1935–1975) launched a radically distinct programme of research in the 1960s that ultimately evolved into CA. Sacks' initial research was based on a corpus of telephone calls to the Los Angeles Suicide Prevention Centre (Sacks, 1992) and he was initially primarily interested in how people describe and manage suicide threats. As he analysed the calls, he became intrigued by the ways callers and call-takers managed everyday activities such as opening their conversations, identifying one another, making requests, and agreeing and disagreeing with each other. This led him to focus on the mundane workings of conversation and to systematically explore, through the analysis of recordings of naturally occurring talk, how people create the kind of orderliness that Garfinkel referred to in their everyday interactions.

In collaboration with Emanuel Schegloff and Gail Jefferson, Sacks went on to develop a unique qualitative methodology, which focuses on the intricate details of the organization of naturally occurring social interactions, as they occur in real time. This involves repeated and detailed analysis of recordings of talk-in-interaction using a unique transcription scheme, devised by Jefferson (2004) to capture the rich detail and complexity of naturally occurring social interactions. In their early studies Sacks and his co-workers focused mainly on recordings of everyday conversations amongst friends, family and acquaintances and, as a result, their approach came to be known as conversation analysis. They investigated phenomena such as storytelling (Sacks, 1974a, 1974b), speaker turn taking in conversation (Sacks, et al., 1974), and opening and closing telephone conversations (Schegloff and Sacks, 1973). Their aim was to establish a 'naturalistic observation discipline which could deal with the details of social action(s) rigorously, and formally' (Sacks et al., 1974).

CA grew steadily in the 1970s, with studies conducted by both researchers who were personally trained by Harvey Sacks as graduate students (see Lerner, 2004) and researchers in the US and the UK who were inspired not only by the early published studies of Sacks, Schegloff and Jefferson but also the unpublished transcripts of Sacks' lectures which were circulated informally prior to their publication in 1992 (Sacks, 1992). Some of these researchers extended the scope of CA by applying its approach and findings to the analysis of interaction in institutional settings 'where more or less official or formal task- or role-based activities are undertaken' (Heritage, 1997: 406). Early CA studies of institutional interactions focused on medical consultations, telephone calls to emergency services, broadcast news interviews, talk in small claims courts, job interviews, psychiatric intake interviews, business meetings and classroom lessons (e.g. see Drew and Heritage, 1992a).

The principles of CA were also extended to the study of forms of human conduct in social interaction other than talk, for example, gaze, gesture and body orientations (e.g. Goodwin, 1981, 1986; Heath, 1986). This involved the use of CA to explore the ways in which nonverbal conduct features in the production and intelligibility of social actions and activities, both in casual conversation and institutional interaction. This focus on the interplay between nonverbal aspects and verbal aspects of interaction was accompanied by the further development of the CA transcription system through the inclusion of notation to track gaze direction, gestures and bodily orientations (see Atkinson and Heritage, 1984). More recently, the principles of CA have been extended to the analysis of technology-mediated interactions such as emails and virtual meetings (e.g. Markman, 2009).

While originally developed from a sociological perspective, CA has subsequently been used by researchers from a range of disciplinary backgrounds, including anthropology, communication, human-computer interaction, medicine, psychology, a variety of linguistic subdisciplines and, as noted, business and management research. Moreover, in addition to North America and the UK, it is now practised in many other countries in Scandinavia, Europe more generally, as well as Asia and Australasia. It has consequently been applied to a substantial number of languages. Indeed, several studies have examined the extent to which specific interactional practices are universal or variable across different cultures and languages (e.g. Kasper and Wagner, 2014).

Outline of the CA Methodology

CA comprises a data-driven methodology which seeks to ground theoretical and analytic claims in the moment-to-moment understandings of their circumstances that participants display to one another during their interactions. CA does not begin with a priori hypotheses, which are then subjected to empirical testing. Rather, CA uses an inductive approach in order to identify the shared methods through which people accomplish social actions and activities. In doing so, it focuses on aspects of linguistic, paralinguistic and visual conduct that can only be systematically examined through repeated inspection of audio or video recordings of naturally occurring encounters. The fundamental aim of CA is to explicate the methods through which people manage their interactions in an orderly, intelligible fashion. CA research reveals what Garkinkel referred to as the tacit '"seen but unnoticed", expected, background features' (Garfinkel, 1967: 35-6) of social and organizational settings which remain largely, if not wholly, unavailable to researchers who rely solely on data generated through observation, interviews or questionnaires.

CA is concerned with the level of detail that can be shown to be relevant to participants themselves. CA studies demonstrate that participants actually orient to the so-called minutiae of talk-in-interaction, including pauses timed to tenths of a second and intakes of breath and the precise placement of overlapping talk. So, for example, if someone issues an invitation, it is by no means uncommon to find them reformulating/moderating their invitation if the invitee has not responded within a fraction of a second. Similarly, perturbations in speech have been shown to be coordinated with the gaze direction of recipients, with speakers cutting off their speech in progress until a recipient resumes eye contact. It is therefore necessary to attend to the apparent minutia of participants' verbal and nonverbal conduct in order to establish the *in situ* social organization of talk-in-interaction because this is the level of detail at which the participants themselves are operating. In CA 'no order of detail can be dismissed a priori as disorderly, accidental, or irrelevant' (Heritage, 1984, p.241).

The basic unit of analysis in CA research is sequences of turns at talk rather than individual utterances (Schegloff, 2007). A sequence is an organized series of turns through which participants accomplish and coordinate an interactional activity. A simple example of a sequence is a question followed by an answer. Other examples are an offer and the decision that is made about it, a complaint and the response to it, and an exchange of greetings.

The approach is qualitative, but generally involves looking across multiple instances in a collection of examples in order to describe generic and stable features of interactional practices that are independent of the particular contextual features of any given situation. In locating and analysing patterns of action and interaction, CA researchers repeatedly replay audio or video recordings of naturally occurring social interactions, carefully transcribing the events. The transcripts capture not only what is said ('the verbal part of the talk'), but also various details of speech production, such as overlapping talk, pauses within and between utterances, stress, pitch and volume. The transcripts may also track visual conduct such as gestures and gaze direction. Consider the following transcript of an extract from a video recording of a medical consultation, in which a doctor is prescribing medication to treat an eye problem, along with tablets for another condition. The patient is standing behind the doctor dressing, as the doctor enters the details required to print a prescription onto a computer-based medical record system.

Extract 1.1 [Based on an extract used in Greatbatch, 2006]
```
 1 Doctor:   Just one tablet a day (1.0) for the: (0.4)
 2           eyes, [see if it'll help the itch.
 3 Patient:        [mm mm
 4          (0.4)
 5          ((Patient sniffs))
 6 Doctor:   It may not help at all we'll have to see.
 7          (.)
 8 Doctor:   I'll just give you twenty for now.
 9          (0.6)
10 Patient:  So they won't clash with one another.
11          (.)
12 Doctor:   No. ((doctor shakes his head))=
13 Patient:  =No. Good ((patient looks away from the doctor))
```

The symbols used in the extract are explained in Box 1.1 below.

Box 1.1   Selected transcription symbols

(0.4)	A number in parenthesis indicates the length of a silence in tenths of a second (e.g. lines 1, 4 and 9)
(.)	A period in parenthesis indicates a silence of less than two tenths of a second (e.g. lines 7 and 11)
[	A left bracket between adjacent lines of concurrent speech indicates the onset of overlap (e.g. lines 2 and 3)
(( ))	Text in double-parenthesis describes nonverbal activity (e.g. lines 5, 12 and 13)
.	A period indicates a falling final intonation contour (e.g. lines 2, 6, 8 and 10)
Word	A word or letter underline indicates speaker emphasis (e.g. line 1)

Using the glossary in Box 1.1 will enable you to see in what ways the transcript represents details of how the doctor and patient speak in overlap, pause within and between turns at talk and communicate non-verbally. We will explain how CA researchers time silences within and between utterances in Chapter 4 when we take you through the steps of conducting a CA study and provide you with a comprehensive glossary of the transcription symbols used in CA, including those for nonverbal conduct.

Outline of the Procedural Steps Involved in Carrying Out a CA Study

CA studies are typically undertaken in a series of 6 overlapping steps, which we summarize below. These are explained in more detail in Chapter 4.

Step 1: Data collection

During this stage, audio or video recordings of naturally social interaction are collected in four main ways. First, a researcher can set up their own audio or video recording equipment to record face-to-face or technologically mediated interactions, including telephone calls, video calls and web-based chats. Second, a researcher can acquire access to recordings made by other people. For example, many organizations – including airlines, banks, insurers, retailers, utility companies and emergency services – record telephone calls to their contact centres for quality assurance and training purposes. Third, a researcher can make recordings of radio or television programmes that include, for example, interactions between prospective investees and 'dragons' in the TV programme *Dragons' Den*, broadcast interviews on business and management-related topics, or press conferences. Fourth, a researcher can download recordings from the web, including speeches and lectures given by business leaders, commentators/experts or management consultants, or debates. In all these cases, CA researchers follow strict ethical guidelines, which are discussed in Chapter 4.

Step 2: Formulation of research questions

CA researchers do not usually start with specific research questions in mind when looking at the data. The early stages of CA research generally involve 'unmotivated looking', with researchers reviewing audio or video recordings in order to establish what is there in terms of content, identify phenomena which strike them as interesting and formulate their initial research questions on the basis of this. For example, in reviewing publicly available news interviews of corporate leaders which focus on their response to a crisis, research questions might arise in relation to how the interviewer's questions are answered or not answered, how aggressive and challenging questions are answered, how accountability, control and leadership are enacted through the responses from the interviewee and so forth. Similarly, in recordings of service encounters a researcher could examine the role of humour and laughter in establishing rapport and securing a purchase.

Step 3: Transcription of data

This stage involves transcribing selected audio-visual data, using the system developed by Gail Jefferson (2004). This system includes a very large number of symbols which allow researchers to capture an incredible amount of detail in their transcripts. This should not put you off. You will most likely only use a small number of the symbols. Many will not be needed for your study because either they refer to aspects of talk that do not arise in your data extracts or are not relevant to your analysis.

You will probably have already noticed that Stage 3 (transcription) could well overlap with Stage 2 (identifying research questions) and Stage 4 (data analysis). This is because as you transcribe your data it is possible that you will refine or even change your research questions as you become increasingly familiar with your data and, as you transcribe, you will inevitably start to analyse the data, noting patterns, similarities and differences, and interesting observations.

Step 4: Data analysis

This stage involves analysing either a single case or, more commonly, collection of examples of the phenomenon that is of interest to the researcher. Repeatedly replaying those elements of the recordings that are of interest to you, you identify the culturally shared methods that participants use to (i) accomplish and coordinate their social actions and (ii) maintain an 'architecture' of publicly displayed and continuously updated intersubjective understanding of their circumstances (Heritage, 1984) as their interactions unfold moment by moment in real time.

Step 5: Identification of contribution to knowledge

During this stage of the research process, you identify how your findings contribute to the literature related to your topic of investigation.

Step 6: Writing up findings

You now write up your findings in your dissertation, using transcripts of extracts from recordings as examples of the phenomena you describe. In so doing you show how your research fills gaps, and builds on and contributes to the relevant literature.

CONVERSATION ANALYSIS WITHIN BUSINESS AND MANAGEMENT RESEARCH

Despite the fact that talk-in-interaction pervades almost every aspect of organizational life, prior to the turn of the century it attracted relatively little consideration in business and management research. Until then it was largely either overlooked or treated as epiphenomenal, or considered in studies of 'communication skill', which pay little, if any, attention to the actual details of naturally occurring talk in organizations (Samra-Fredericks, 1998). Research in the field of organizational communication was (and to some extent still is) associated with quantitative analyses based on questionnaires, experimental methods and interviews.

Since the turn of the century, however, there has been a move in business and management research towards micro-analytical studies of naturally occurring talk in organizations. This is part of a broader trend in business and management research towards examining more directly what actually takes place in organizations and focusing on what organizational members do when interacting with each other and how they do what they do. There is growing emphasis therefore on the need to analyse the in situ accomplishment of activities such as leadership in real time through fine-grained analyses of audio or video recordings (and transcripts thereof) of naturally occurring interaction (Clifton, 2014).

The growing focus on studying and understanding the details of talk-in-interaction in organizations is to a large extent methodologically based on CA (Asmuß and Svennevig, 2009). Within business and management research CA has been used in studies in organizations of varying sizes across the private, public and not-for-profit sectors in the UK, Continental Europe, the US, Canada, Australasia and Japan. These studies have focused on a diverse array of topics, including leadership and influencing, strategy meetings, decision-making, recruitment interviews, performance reviews, and service encounters. They clearly demonstrate that CA can make significant theoretical contributions to a range of debates and literatures within management research. Together with CA studies of institutional talk, this body of work provides a rich repository of research findings on talk in organizational settings that you can draw on in your research.

OUTLINE OF THIS BOOK

Having introduced you to CA and its place in business and management, the remainder of this book will explain the method in more depth, to enable you to use it successfully in your own work. In Chapter 2 we will consider the philosophical underpinnings of CA, paying particular attention to its roots in ethnomethodology. Chapter 3 provides a detailed discussion of the CA methodology, including both single case and multiple case analyses. Chapter 4 provides a detailed account of the steps involved in using CA, expanding on the summary presented in this chapter and illustrating the steps by reference an example of how we have used CA in our own research. To help you find your way around the literature, we provide an overview of CA research in business and management studies in Chapter 5. Finally, in Chapter 6 we evaluate the strengths and limitations of CA.

CHAPTER SUMMARY

Within this chapter we have:

- Introduced the general approach and findings of CA
- Described CA's historical development
- Outlined the key procedural steps involved in carrying out a CA study
- Discussed the use of CA within business and management research
- Provided an outline of the remainder of this book.

2

UNDERSTANDING CONVERSATION ANALYSIS

In this chapter we explore CA's theoretical roots and outline its core theoretical assumptions. It is important that you understand these in order to:

- Decide whether CA fits with your research interests
- Ensure that CA's theoretical stance is consistent with your own perspective
- Ensure that, if you use CA, your analysis is consistent with the expectations of the intellectual community, including practising conversation analysts.

We will begin by explaining how the work of the sociologists Erving Goffman and Harold Garfinkel influenced the development of CA. We will then turn to consider the role of theorising in CA before outlining the key theoretical assumptions on which CA research is based.

THEORETICAL BACKGROUND

CA emerged in the late 1960s in an intellectual context shaped by the perspectives developed by the American sociologists Erving Goffman (1922–1982) and Harold Garfinkel (1917–2011). Harvey Sacks (like his close collaborator Emanuel Schegloff) was a sociology student of Goffman at the University of California, Berkeley and was influenced by Goffman's theoretical position in relation to the importance of every-day social interaction. Crucially, Sacks also had an ongoing intellectual and personal relationship with Garfinkel that began in 1959 and was sustained through the early

1970s (Schegloff, 1992d: xiii). As we indicated in Chapter 1, CA emerged to a significant degree through Sacks' engagement with Garfinkel's ethnomethodological studies of the practices and methods through which people render everyday social actions and activities intelligible. CA is widely regarded as an offshoot of ethnomethodology, although the relationship between CA and ethnomethodology has become less clear-cut over the last 50 years, as CA has evolved and cascaded across a range of academic disciplines and fields of study.

Erving Goffman: The Interaction Order

Erving Goffman was one of the most perceptive sociological observers of the dynamics of everyday life and his contribution to sociology is immense. Goffman's core achievement (see Goffman, 1955, 1983) was to establish that social interaction is a form of social institution in its own right that can be analysed like other social institutions, such as education, the family and religion. Goffman described the institution of social interaction as 'the interaction order', a body of largely tacit conventions (such as salutations) that members of society are normally expected to follow when interacting with each other in face-to-face situations involving two or more people (Goffman, 1983). For Goffman, these conventions (norms and rituals) constitute the grammar of social interaction in that they structure the relationship between the social actions of people who are in each other's presence. According to Goffman, social interactions are driven not by social actors' individual intentions and motivations but rather by their management of these situational conventions. Goffman (1967: 2) used the following dictum to summarize his stance: 'I assume that the proper study of interaction is not the individual and his psychology, but rather the syntactical relations amongst the acts of different persons mutually present to one another.' Goffman argued that the interaction order occupies a foundational status in relation to other institutions in society – including political, economic, educational and legal social institutions – because the operations of other institutions are largely transacted through the practices that comprise the institution of social interaction.

Goffman's brilliant insights influenced the early development of CA in that they provided legitimacy for the study of the details of everyday social interaction. His perspective remained distinct from CA, however. One reason for this is that Goffman's work primarily involved theoretical analyses, in which he used data/evidence in a rather loose manner to illustrate the conceptual schemes he devised for ordering the social world (Schegloff, 1988). This stands in marked contrast to CA, which emphasizes the importance of rigorous empirical analysis of real-time audio or video recordings of naturally occurring interaction and eschews a priori theorizing by researchers.

Another important difference between Goffman's work and CA is that whereas CA immediately made use of audio and video recording technologies, Goffman disavowed both. Virtually none of his examples are transcripts of recorded interactions of naturally occurring talk-in-interaction, the major exception being his essay on radio talk (Goffman, 1981). Goffman continued to rely on observation, field notes and excerpted materials from reports of others, including journalists, novelists and playwrights. In some instances, he also used hypothetically constructed examples.

Harold Garfinkel: Practical Theorizing in Everyday Practices

As we noted in Chapter 1, Harold Garfinkel (1967) was the founder of ethnomethodology, an approach to studying social life that offers a distinctive perspective on the nature and origins of social order by focusing on the tacit shared methods of practical reasoning ('ethno methods') that social actors use to achieve shared understandings of the social world. Ethnomethodology rejects 'top-down' theories that explain the organization of everyday life in terms of larger overarching cultural or social structural phenomena. Adopting a 'bottom-up' approach, ethnomethodology focuses on the emergent achievement of social order that results from the concerted efforts of social actors within everyday encounters. This involves analysts revealing the multiplicity of tacit methods of reasoning (or procedures) that social actors use to produce and interpret social actions, situations, and structures and to thereby maintain shared understandings of the social world. As Heritage (2001: 913) observes: 'These methods are procedural in character, they are socially shared and they are ceaselessly used during every waking moment to recognize ordinary social objects and events.'

Social science is generally characterized by the adherence to particular research paradigms and general theories which are underpinned by distinctive philosophical assumptions regarding ontology (assumptions about the nature of reality), epistemology (how the researcher comes to understand that reality through the development of knowledge) and methodology (the specific methods that can be used to try to find out about the world). Box 2.1 below summarizes five common research paradigms in the social sciences.

Ethnomethodology is commonly regarded as a form of phenomenology or social constructionism, which can be located within the interpretivist paradigm. However, Garfinkel completely rejected this characterization of his approach to the study of everyday life, and he objected to all attempts to locate ethnomethodology within the mainstream research paradigms in the social sciences. Garfinkel adopted a principled agnosticism with regard to research paradigms and social theory, such as those included in Box 2.1; he referred to this as adopting an attitude of 'ethnomethodological indifference'. Garfinkel's aim was to elucidate the practices and methods through which people produce and interpret social actions and activities in particular settings without distorting them through the use of concepts, which a social theorist might bring to the analysis from outside those settings.

Table 2.1 Common research paradigms

Paradigm or philosophical framework	Ontology Assumptions about the status of social reality	Epistemology Assumptions about the grounds of knowledge	Methodology The way in which research is to be conducted
Positivism	Realist Assumes that there is an objective social reality 'out there' that is independent from human perceptual or cognitive structures	Representational Assumes people can objectively observe the social world	Hypothetico-deductive Assumes that science should focus exclusively on directly observable phenomena, without any reference to the subjective Generally involves testing theories and hypotheses, using quantitative methods
Qualitative neo-positivism	Realist Assumes that there is an objective social reality 'out there' that is independent from human perceptual or cognitive structures	Representational Assumes people can objectively or neutrally observe the social world	Qualitative Rejects two key aspects of positivism: the use of hypothetico-deductive methodology and the exclusion of the subjective as meaningless Involves the use of qualitative methods to investigate intersubjective cultural processes by gathering facts from what is purported to be a readily observable external social world
Interpretivism	Relativist Assumes that what we regard as social reality is a social construction built upon the perceptions and actions of social actors, although social actors are not generally aware of their role in these processes	Subjectivist Rejects the possibility of neutral observation and focuses instead on human interpretations and understandings	Qualitative Focuses on the interpretations and meanings individuals give to social situations
Critical Realism	Realist Assumes that there is an objective social reality 'out there' that is independent from human perceptual or cognitive structures	Post-positivist Assumes that our ability to apprehend social reality is imperfect and shaped by our cultural assumptions. Claims about reality may therefore be more or less accurate	Quantitative and qualitative Stresses the importance of multiple measures and observations and the use of triangulation across these multiple sources in order to develop descriptions that are as objective as possible
Critical theory	Historical/Relativist Assumes there is a social reality that is socially constructed and taken to be natural or real, which is shaped over time by ideological, social, cultural, political and economic forces and values	Modified subjectivist Assumes that knowledge is not value free. It is socially constructed and influenced by power relations from within society	Qualitative Oriented towards critiquing and changing society, using qualitative methods

From Garfinkel's seminal work, CA adopted the notion that people unavoidably use and rely on a range of tacit practices and procedures (ethnomethods) to produce and recognize mutually intelligible contributions to social interaction. Moreover, like ethnomethodology, CA adopted a 'bottom-up' approach to research and an aversion to a priori theorizing (Maynard and Clayman, 1991). However, the question of how closely CA and ethnomethodology are now connected is open to debate. The fact that CA is concerned with building a naturalistic, observation-based empirical science of human social interaction has attracted criticism from some ethnomethodologists who suggest that this is inconsistent with ethnomethodology's core principles. Moreover, the subsequent development of CA research suggests that it has evolved partially independently of ethnomethodology. As Maynard and Clayman (2003: 176) observe:

> Substantively, ethnomethodology's broad concern with diverse forms of practical reasoning and embodied action contrasts with the conversation analytic focus on the comparatively restricted domain of talk-in-interaction and its various constituent activity systems (e.g. turn taking, sequencing, repair, gaze direction, institutional specializations). Methodologically, ethnomethodology's use of ethnography and quasi-experimental demonstrations contrasts with the emphasis on audio- and videorecordings of naturally occurring interaction within CA.

Ten Have (2012: Abstract) summarizes the relationship between CA and ethnomethodology in the following terms:

> There can be hardly any doubt that ethnomethodology has been a major influence in the emergence of conversation analysis (CA) as a unique perspective in the human sciences. Gradually, however, the two seem to have drifted apart. The current situation is ambiguous: For some of its practitioners, CA is still part of the ethnomethodological movement, while many others treat it as an independent pursuit.

Regardless of the precise nature of the relationship between CA and ethnomethodology, as Maynard and Clayman (1991: 397) conclude, 'bonds between the two areas run deep'.

THEORIZING IN CA

In adopting a 'bottom-up' approach to research and theorizing, CA researchers argue against a priori speculation and 'premature' theorizing in favour of detailed examination of participants' concrete actions. As noted in Chapter 1, the actual and immediate conduct of speakers is treated as the central resource out of which analysis should develop. CA thus backgrounds analysts' theoretical concerns and concentrates instead on participants' orientations. As Schegloff (1997, 1999a, 1999b) argues, from the perspective of CA all interpretations must be grounded first in the actual talk and practices of the participants. The aim of the researcher should be to avoid applying theoretical frameworks to understand and explain aspects of social interaction; instead the researcher should focus exclusively on those things that are demonstrably oriented to by the partici-pants themselves. Thus, as Maynard and Clayman (2003: 176) observe: 'Although conversation analysts are not averse to advancing theoretical claims, often of a highly general nature (Wilson and Zimmerman 1979: 67), every effort is made to ground such claims in the observable orientations that interactants themselves display to one other.'

In CA research, then, analysis never begins with explicit theoretical engagement by the researcher. Moreover, CA practitioners only invoke social categories such as gender, race and ethnicity insofar as they are oriented to by the participants in their talk. In other words, the analyst treats as relevant only that which the participants themselves display as relevant in their interaction. For example, in an analysis of a conversation between an elderly disabled male and a young female, the social con-structs of age, disability and gender would only be used if it could be demonstrated that the participants themselves are orienting to them in their talk and/or nonver-bal conduct. The analyst would have to show that these considerations coincide with the actual orientations of the participants who are performing the social actions and using the interactional practices that are being studied.

In summary, CA researchers seek to:

- Develop theoretical claims on the basis of rigorous analysis of recordings of natu-rally occurring social interaction
- Ground theoretical claims in the observable orientations that participants them-selves display to each other as their interactions unfold in real time.

CORE THEORETICAL CLAIMS

Early CA research developed three theoretical claims about the social organization of talk-in-interaction that underpin all CA research and are intimately connected with the research techniques that CA researchers use (Heritage, 1984 (Ch. 8); Hutchby and Wooffitt, 1998). These theoretical propositions concern: (1) the performance of social actions in turns at talk, (2) the structural organization of social actions in talk-in-interaction and (3) the creation and maintenance of shared intersubjective understandings through talk-in-interaction.

1. Talk is Action

CA is based on the empirically derived theoretical proposition that when people talk to each other they perform social actions. Readily recognizable examples of social actions accomplished through talk include asking and answering (or declining to answer) a question, agreeing or disagreeing with someone, complaining, apologizing, making an invitation, declining an invitation, praising someone, thanking someone, telling and receiving news, and so on. This theoretical proposition chimes with the insights of ordinary language philosophers (Austin, 1962; Searle, 1969; Wittgenstein, 1953) who argued that everyday language involves the performance of social actions; however, CA adopted it on the basis of empirical analysis rather than as a result of philosophical considerations.

2. Action is Structurally Organized

Through detailed studies of recordings of naturally occurring talk, CA researchers have shown that, in accomplishing social actions, participants orient to rules and structures that facilitate the production and recognition of intelligible social actions. These rules and structures mainly concern the sequential relations between actions that are accomplished through turns at talk. Single acts are parts of larger, structurally organized entities referred to as sequences (Schegloff, 1995). The most basic and important sequence is called an 'adjacency pair' (Schegloff and Sacks, 1973), which is a sequence of two actions in which the first action ('first pair part'), performed by one participant, invites a particular type of second action ('second pair part'), to be performed by another participant. Typical examples of adjacency pairs include question–answer, invitation–acceptance/declination and request–grant/refusal. The relationship between the first and second pair parts of adjacency pairs is normative: if the second pair part is not forthcoming, the first speaker may, for example, justifiably repeat the first action, complain or seek explanations for why the second action is missing (Atkinson and Drew, 1979: 52-7). As we shall see in Chapter 3, there are other types of sequential structure too. Basically, any current turn at talk (action performed by a speaker) sets the coordinates for the relevant choices for the next turn (Heritage and Atkinson, 1984: 6). Of course, current actions never determine the next action (e.g. asking someone a question doesn't guarantee that they will answer it), but the next action is always produced and understood by reference to its occurrence at its particular slot in the conversation (i.e. after the current action).

3. Talk Creates and Maintains Intersubjective Reality

CA studies have also revealed how participants create and maintain a framework of intersubjective understanding on a moment-by-moment basis as their interactions unfold in real time (Heritage and Atkinson, 1984: 11). CA focuses solely on meanings and understandings that are displayed through conversational action, and remains 'agnostic' with regards to participants' inner feelings, plans, intentions, motivations and the like (Heritage, 1984).

The intersubjective understandings that participants create and maintain at the 'conversational surface' concern:

- The social actions that participants perform in their turns at talk: CA proceeds on the basis that each and every turn at talk displays some level of understanding of the preceding turn, which the first speaker may subsequently accept as adequate/satisfactory or, alternatively, incorrect or problematic (Schegloff, 1992c) – for example, by saying 'I didn't mean to criticize you, I was just explaining the situation I am in.'
- The current state of the talk (Heritage and Atkinson, 1984: 10): for example, speakers display their understanding of when it is appropriate to initiate new lines of talk or initiate closure of an interaction. They may also display their understanding that their interaction is taking place to accomplish institutional activities (e.g. a medical consultation, a job interview or a performance appraisal review) and shape their actions accordingly.

THE USE OF CA IN DISCIPLINES AND FIELDS OF STUDY

Although CA emerged within the discipline of sociology, as noted in the previous chapter, it is now used by scholars operating in a host of disciplines and subject areas, including linguistics, psychology and anthropology, human-computer interaction (HCI), computer-supported cooperative work (CSCW) and business and management, amongst others. This has meant that in some cases researchers who do not necessarily have a strong link with sociology or ethnomethodology have made use of CA in their research. Nonetheless, studies that present themselves as involving the use of CA are generally underpinned by the philosophical and theoretical commitments introduced in this chapter. This applies to most, if not all, CA studies that have been conducted in the field of business and management research. As we shall see in Chapter 5, while these studies are formulated in terms of key issues in business and management research, they remain committed to the underlying assumptions of CA. Indeed, it is the fact that they do so which leads to them offering unique insights into the issues that are of concern to business and management researchers.

If you do come across studies that are described as CA but do not seem to be entirely consistent with the theoretical and methodological considerations we have identified, you should take this into account when assessing the strength and relevance of the work in question. Specifically, you should ask: Are the data of naturally occurring interactions? How were they collected? How might restrictions related to access and the sensitivity of the interaction being recorded impact on the analysis? Furthermore, and this is a common failing of researchers using CA for the first time, to what extent is the analysis foregrounding what is said and how participants orient themselves to each other's turns rather than ex ante conceptual considerations? As we have emphasized earlier, CA is grounded in the practices and understandings participants display through their respective turns at talk at the 'conversational surface'. Researchers using CA have to constantly ensure they are not moving to speculations about the internal motivations and cognitive states of the participants.

CHAPTER SUMMARY

Within this chapter we have highlighted the following points in relation to the development of CA and the theoretical assumptions on which it is based:

- CA emerged out of ethnomethodology, which seeks to understand social life in terms of participants' own orientations and practices without recourse to theoretical concepts developed by social scientists outside the particular settings and situations that are being studied.
- CA is also indebted to Erving Goffman who established that social interaction is not only a social institution in its own right but also underpins all other social institutions. However, CA is distinct from Goffman's approach because it insists on the use of audio and video recordings of naturally occurring talk-in-interaction and eschews a priori theorizing by researchers.
- For CA, it is necessary to remain focused on the practices, orientations and understandings that participants in interaction use and display as their interactions unfold. The analyst should therefore avoid imposing or relying upon 'external' academic theories and concepts in order to explain what is taking place in an interactional context. The theoretical insights generated by CA are firmly rooted in empirical analyses.
- CA studies share at least three basic theoretical propositions, which emerged from rigorous empirical studies of recordings of naturally occurring social interactions:
    - Talk is a vehicle through which people accomplish social actions
    - Participants in interaction render social actions in talk intelligible by orienting to tacit structures of action, which are termed sequences
    - Participants create and maintain a framework of publicly displayed intersubjective understanding at the conversational surface.
- CA is unique in the way in which it reveals how 'action', 'structure' and 'intersubjectivity' are practically achieved and managed in talk-in-interaction.

3

BASIC COMPONENTS OF CONVERSATION ANALYSIS

In this chapter we examine CA methodology in more detail. We will consider why CA researchers insist on the use of audio and video recordings to study talk in interaction and discuss how they approach the tasks of analysing and transcribing these data. The chapter is structured under the following headings:

1. Using recording technologies
2. Formulating research questions
3. Transcribing recordings
4. Focus of analysis
5. Modes of analysis
6. Constraints on analysis
7. Analysing talk in institutional settings.

USING RECORDING TECHNOLOGIES

CA researchers argue that, for the analysis of social interaction, audio and video recordings of naturally occurring social interaction offer several important advantages over alternative sources of data, such as responses to questionnaires, interview data, observational studies relying on field notes or coding procedures, idealized or invented examples based on the researcher's own native intuitions, and experimental methodologies. These advantages are as follows:

- They provide the researcher with repeatable access to the richness, complexity and specific details of real world actions, allowing particular events to be scrutinized repeatedly and subjected to detailed inspection: 'a microscope with which to study human life' (Greatbatch et al., 1995: 202).
- They provide some guarantee that analytic conclusions will not be based upon idiosyncratic intuition, selective attention, selective recollection or experimental research design.
- They provide 'raw' data to which a range of analytic interests can be applied, unconstrained by the concerns of a particular research study.
- They enable other researchers within the scientific community to evaluate the strength of particular analyses with respect to the original data and thereby provide an important constraint on the quality and rigour of findings.
- They provide readers of research reports with direct access to the data about which analytic claims are being made, thereby making them available for public scrutiny in a way that further minimizes the influence of individual preconceptions (Heritage and Atkinson, 1984).

Thus, audio and video recordings of naturally occurring social interaction are viewed by CA researchers as offering access to actual events as they happened in real time, whereas other forms of data are seen as being too much a product of the researcher's or informant's idiosyncrasies, selective recollections and preconceptions of what is probable or important (Heritage and Atkinson, 1984: 2-3).

Nonetheless, CA researchers recognize that there are issues relating to the validity of audio and video recordings of real world events that must be borne in mind when conducting a CA study. In particular, there is the problem of 'reactivity', which refers to the possibility that the presence of a video camera or an audio recorder can influence the behaviour of those being recorded and thereby undermine the quality of at least some of the video or audio data that is collected.

Some social scientists who specialize in conducting video-based studies, which draw on CA and ethnomethodology, have addressed this issue empirically by specifically identifying the influence of video recording on research subjects (e.g. participant orientations to the camera) rather than simply removing examples of 'reactivity' from their datasets as 'bad data' (e.g. see Knoblauch et al., 2006; Heath et al., 2010). Heath et al. (2010) suggest that by analysing the moments where the camera seems to have had an effect on participants' conduct, they are able to understand how and when reactivity arises and its impact on the video data they collect for their research studies. They find that the extent of any reactivity on video data varies depending on: how video cameras are used, for example, whether they are fixed or mobile/roaming (Heath et al., 2010); the length of time over which the video recording takes place, with reactivity possibly reducing over time as people become used to being video recorded and less aware of video cameras (Knoblauch et al., 2006); and whether the research context is one where people are regularly observed/recorded. On the basis of having conducted numerous video-based studies, Heath et al. (2010: 49) conclude that the issue of 'reactivity' is often exaggerated:

> Throughout our studies of a diverse range of settings and activities we found that within a short time, the camera is 'made at home'. It rarely receives notice or attention and there is little empirical evidence that it has transformed the ways in which participants accomplish actions.

Heath et al. (2010: 49) also draw attention to the fact that '(A)ssessing the influence of any method of data collection and its impact on the quality of the research data collected is an important issue for any research.' On the basis of our experience of collecting video and audio recordings of interactions in a variety of institutional settings, we believe that Heath et al.'s conclusions regarding the use of video are correct and that they also apply in the case of audio recordings.

Of course, CA research is not always based on the analysis of recordings that have been made specifically for research studies. Sometimes CA studies focus on recordings that that have been made by organizations for quality, training or legal purposes; for example, there are studies of audio recordings provided by telemedicine providers, emergency services, financial services call centres, and customer helplines. Because these recordings have not been specifically collected for research purposes, any examples of reactivity by the participants are constituent elements of the interactions being studied rather than the result of the 'interventions' of a researcher or research team. This is also the case when data comprise recordings of naturally occurring events – such as debates, interviews and speeches – that have been made for distribution via television, radio and the Internet and can be accessed through, for example, Google, YouTube, TED Talks or the websites of radio and television broadcasters.

FORMULATING RESEARCH QUESTIONS

CA studies begin with what Sacks (Sacks, 1992: Lecture 5 [1967]) described as 'unmotivated looking' of recorded interaction with the objective of noticing something that strikes the researcher as interesting about it. Once a researcher has noticed something of interest, they assemble a collection of possible instances which they subsequently analyse on a case-by-case basis. Some researchers do, however, start out with more or less clearly defined questions. This is often because they have an ongoing interest in a particular area (e.g. interruptions/overlapping talk), which may initially have been sparked by unmotivated inspection of recordings in an earlier study, by reading other people's publications, or by practical concerns, such as improving understanding of how clinicians communicate diagnoses or information about prescribed treatments.

Regardless of whether they adopt more or less clearly defined research questions at the outset of their studies, all CA researchers remain open to revising their research questions as they become increasingly familiar with their data.

TRANSCRIBING RECORDINGS

Transcription is central to the process of reviewing and analysing audio and video recordings in CA research. CA transcriptions represent recorded material in written form, which enables researchers to attend to details of talk in interaction that might otherwise escape their attention and which would be unavailable for systematic analysis. CA transcripts can also provide researchers with access to the details of a wide range of interactional episodes, which can then be examined for comparative purposes at a fine level of granularity. Furthermore, as noted, selected extracts from transcripts can be included as examples of interactional phenomena in CA research papers and reports, providing readers with a way of checking the analysis presented.

CA researchers are only too aware that their transcripts cannot represent recordings of naturally occurring interactions in their *full* detail. Transcripts are always and necessarily selective. As noted in Chapter 1, the transcription system used in CA is specifically designed to capture the sequential features of talk – that is, how turns at talk are organized as a series of interconnected actions in successive turns at talk. The choice of which details are included in a CA transcript is therefore largely shaped by a concern with the sequential organization of talk.

FOCUS OF ANALYSIS

CA researchers follow a number of basic principles, which together form an 'analytic mentality' which structures the ways in which they approach the task of analysing their data. These basic principles, which we have touched upon in the preceding chapters, can be summarized as follows:

- There is 'order at all points' in talk-in-interaction. Wherever you focus your analytic gaze, you will find phenomena that are systematically organized by the participants themselves.
- No order of detail should be dismissed a priori as disorderly, accidental or irrelevant.
- Contributions to interaction should not be analysed in isolation because they are both context shaped and context renewing. They are context shaped because they cannot be adequately understood except by reference to the sequential environment in which they occur and in which the participants design them to

occur. They are context renewing because they also form part of the sequential environment in which a next contribution will occur.

- Analysis should be data driven and should not be constrained by a priori theoretical assumptions, regarding, for example, the importance or relevance of gender, power or race.

In applying these principles, as we have already noted, CA researchers focus on sequence organization, which refers to the ways in which participants link their turns at talk to each other as a coherent series of interrelated communicative actions. A sequence is an ordered series of turns through which participants accomplish and coordinate an interactional activity. A question followed by an answer is an example of a sequence. Other examples are a request and the decision that is made about it, an offer and its acceptance or declination, and a criticism and the reply to it. The examples we have given are in fact instances of a two-part sequence type involving tight sequential constraints, known as adjacency pairs (Schegloff, 1968; Schegloff and Sacks, 1973), which are a pervasive feature of talk-in-interaction in both conversational and institutional settings. As defined by Schegloff and Sacks (1973: 295-6), adjacency pairs are sequences of two utterances that are: (i) adjacent, (ii) produced by different speakers, (iii) ordered as a first part and a second part, and (iv) typed, so that a first part requires a particular second part (or range of second parts) (Heritage, 1984: 246). The occurrence of the first part of an adjacent pair (e.g. a question) establishes a strong constraint (known as conditional relevance) that it should be followed by an appropriate second pair part (in the case of a question, an answer), produced by the recipient(s). If the conditionally relevant second pair part is absent, then this is a noticeable and accountable matter (Schegloff, 1968).

Conversation analysts draw attention to several kinds of evidence for the proposal that speakers orient to the conditional relevance of a second pair part following the production of a first. One type of evidence is that, in the event of first pair parts failing to elicit a response, speakers often propose that a second pair part is accountably due, and hence noticeably absent, through the production of repeats of their original utterances. This is the case, for example, in Extract 3.1 and Extract 3.2 below where, in the absence of response to an initial question, 'A' and 'Ch' respectively repeat and then, in the further absence of response, re-repeat their questions in truncated forms. In each instance the re-repeat is successful in eliciting the looked-for answer.

Extract 3.1 (Atkinson and Drew, 1979: 52)

A: Is there something bothering you or not?

      (1.0)

A: Yes or no

      (1.5)

A: Eh?

B: No

Extract 3.2 (Atkinson and Drew, 1979: 52)

Ch: Have to cut these Mummy

    (1.3)

Ch: Won't we Mummy

    (1.5)

Ch: Won't we

M: Yes

Another type of evidence for the normative character of adjacency pairs is that the absence of the second part of a pair is a matter about which complaints are regularly made. Thus, the arrowed utterances in Extracts 3.3 and 3.4 can all be heard as complaints of a kind about the failure of participants to answer questions:

Extract 3.3 (Atkinson and Drew, 1979: 54)

A: What did you think then (.) Pete?

    (5.7)

A: Eh

    (16.5)

B: ->Don't all shout at once

Extract 3.4 (Atkinson and Drew, 1979: 54)

(A's initial question in this extract is addressed to the 'Dave' named in C's utterance, and in B's enquiry)

A: So you:re just being awkward for the sake of it

    (1.8)

A: Why're you being awkward then?

    (1.8)

A: Eh

    (8.4)

C: -> You know summat Dave, the other day when I was (.) saying

and I was asking a question to everybody and you butted in

before I asked you and you says oh you never ask me

anything. And when I do ask you, you don't say nowt

(2.5)

B: -> Are you listening Dave?

D: Yeah

A third type of evidence is that the non-producers of second pair parts themselves frequently attend to the normative accountability of the adjacency pair structure. So, for example, although the questions in Extracts 3.5 and 3.6 are not answered, they are responded to, with the second speaker in each case offering an account for the non-production of an answer.

Extract 3.5 (Heritage, 1984: 249)

M: What happened at (.) wo:rk. At Bullock's this evening. =

P: ->.hhhh Well I don't know:::w::.

Extract 3.6 (Heritage, 1984: 250)

J: But the train goes. Does th' train go o:n th' boa:t?

M: ->.hh Coh I've no idea:. She ha:sn't sai:d.

Adjacency pair sequences can be expanded in a variety of ways, through pre-expansion, insertion expansions and post-expansions. A pre-expansion involves a sequence that prepares the way for a base first-pair part of an adjacency pair. For example, consider the cases that follow:

Extract 3.7 (Atkinson and Drew, 1979: 253)

A: Whatcha doin'?

B: Nothin'

A: Wanna drink?

Extract 3.8 (Atkinson and Drew, 1979: 143)

C: How ya doin' =

= say what'r you doing?

R: Well we're going out. Why?

C: Oh, I was just gonna say came out and came over here and talk this evening, but if you're going out you can't very well do that.

In each of these cases the initial utterances are transparently preliminaries directed at establishing whether a projected invitation is desired, appropriate or relevant and the second speakers attend to them as such. Thus, in Extract 3.7, B's 'nothing' is hearable not as a literal answer to A's enquiry, but rather as giving a 'go ahead' for the production of the talk that it prefigures. Similarly, in Extract 3.8, R, in requesting that C detail the motive he had in producing his question, plainly displays that he is attending to its prefatory character.

Insert expansions of adjacency pairs intervene between first and second pair parts. These expansions are either backward looking (addressing some issue with a first pair part) or forward looking (preliminary to, and often conditional to, a response). Extract 3.9 provides an example of a forward looking insert expansion of an invitation–acceptance/rejection adjacency pair, with speaker B asking for additional information before responding to speaker A's invitation.

Extract 3.9 (Schegloff, 1972: 78)

A: Are you coming tonight?

B: Can I bring a guest?

A: Sure.

B: I'll be there.

Post-expansion of adjacency pairs sequence often involves response tokens which offer a reaction to a response to a first pair part. Examples include 'Oh' (Heritage, 1984), 'Okay' (Beach, 1993) and 'Great'. An example is shown in Extract 3.10. Here, Carol responds to Gen's answer to her question by saying 'oh', a change-of-state token which treats the question as adequately answered (Stivers, 2013).

Extract 3.10 (Stivers 2013: 198)

Carol: How long will she hafta stay in thuh ho:[spital.

Gen: [It could

         be uh wee:k.=hhh

Carol: SCT ^Oh^:.

Gen: °Yeah:. so_°.hhh ((move to next topic by Gen))

Other types of sequence are less tightly constrained than adjacency pairs. If we consider social actions such as assessments, noticings and other 'comments', we see that although they are commonly responded to, there are times when they are given no response at all. Moreover, this nonresponse does not generally appear to be treated as problematic. Thus, these social actions are not treated as normatively requiring a particular type of response.

Sequences are the core unit of analysis in all CA research. There are other levels of analysis – lexical choice, turn design and the overall structural organization of interactions. However, analysis of these phenomena remains rooted in sequential analysis. Lexical choice and turn design are analysed within the sequential contexts in which they occur, rather than in isolation. The overall structural organization of interactions is considered in terms of how sequences of action cohere.

MODES OF ANALYSIS

There are two kinds of CA studies: collection studies and single case analyses.

Collection Studies

In a collection study, the researcher generalizes the results of a case-by-case analysis of a collection of instances of a specific type of action/activity. All cases in a collection of examples are compared with regard to some feature by describing how, and the extent to which, they are the same, similar or different. So, for example, if you had recordings of calls to a utility company's call centre and became interested in how complaints are managed, you would begin by identifying and building a collection of episodes that involve callers making complaints, which you would then analyse in order to identify similarities and differences in the ways in which the complaints are introduced and managed.

Collection studies have two phases (Heritage, 1995). In the first phase, analysts identify regularities with regard to some aspect of verbal and/or nonverbal interaction in their database. This could involve, for example, how interactions are opened or closed, how topics are introduced and changed (and by whom), how disagreements are managed, how proposals are presented and responded to, and so on. In a second phase, researchers seek to establish whether the participants observably orient to the pattern they have identified. This is accomplished by using a procedure known as deviant case analysis (Schegloff, 1968). In undertaking deviant case analysis, researchers focus on cases in which participants depart from a described pattern in order to establish whether this is treated as unusual, unexpected, problematic or, more generally, accountable. As Heritage (1995: 399) observes: 'Used in this way, deviant case analysis is an important resource for determining whether the basic pattern simply embodies an empirical regularity that happens to occur, or whether it involves something that is oriented to as a normative interactional procedure.'

This form of 'pattern and deviant case' analysis (Heritage 1995: 399) may validate described patterns of interaction by demonstrating that participants actually orient to them. If it does not do so, researchers have to change tack by modifying their analysis. Although some analysts use quantification when describing regularities in interaction, they still use deviant case analysis to demonstrate that participants themselves observably orient to these regularities. Our earlier discussion of adjacency pairs provides an illustration of deviant case analysis. Notice how we demonstrated that participants orient to the adjacency pair structure by considering 'deviant cases' in which second pair parts are *not* produced immediately following first pair parts.

As an example of a collection study, Box 3.1 provides a summary of Pomerantz's influential research on agreements and disagreements with assessments in ordinary conversation.

Box 3.1   Research on agreeing and disagreeing with assessments

In the 1970s Anita Pomerantz (1975, 1978, 1984) examined the alternative actions of agreeing and disagreeing with assessments in mundane conversation in the United States. She found that these actions are routinely accomplished in distinctive ways. Whereas agreements are normally performed directly and with a minimum of delay, disagreements are often delayed from early positioning within turns and sequences and accomplished in mitigated forms.

Disagreements may be delayed as a result of speakers delaying the initiation of their turns at talk, as in Extract 3.11 where speaker B delays the production of their disagreement with A's negative assessment of the weather by pausing before beginning to speak (notice the six tenths of a second's silence after A's assessment).

Extract 3.11 [NB:IV:II-1]

A: God izn' it <u>dreary</u>

(0.6)

B: [.hh- It's <u>warm</u> though.

A: [You know I don't think-

Disagreements are also regularly delayed in conversation through the production of utterances, such as requests for clarification and questioning repeats, which initiate repairs on problems in hearing and/or understanding prior talk. So, for example, in the following extract, due to the production of a request for clarification ('I sound ha:ppy?') by A, A's disagreement ('No') is produced not in the turn adjacent to B's assessment (y-Yih sound HA:PPY, hh) which established the relevance of agreement/disagreement, but rather in a later turn.

Extract 3.12 [TG:1]

B: Why what's the mattuh with y-Yih

    sou[nd HA:PPY, hh

A: [Nothing.

A: I sound ha:p[py?

B: [Ye:uh

    (0.3)

A: No:.

In addition to being delayed sequentially by pre-turn initiation gaps (as in Extract 3.11) and/or pre-disagreement turns (as in 3.12), disagreements in conversation are also frequently delayed and mitigated within the turns in which they occur. So, for example, disagreement components are often delayed and mitigated by 'agreement prefaces', as in Extract 3.13 in which W prefaces her disagreement with L ('but it doesn't do the job') with an agreement component ('Oh it c'n be quicker')

Extract 3.13 [MC:1:13]

L: I know but I, I- I still say that the sewing machine's quicker.

W: Oh it c'n be quicker but it doesn't do the jo:b.

The fact that disagreements are routinely delayed in conversation operates to reduce the likelihood of an as-yet-unstated disagreement materializing. This is because, as is illustrated in Extract 3.14, a speaker may analyse the occurrence of one or more of the devices associated with the delaying of disagreements (in this case silence) as implicating an as-yet-unstated disagreement and, having done so, attempt to forestall its anticipated production by backing away from a prior assertion/assessment.

Extract 3.14 [SBL:3.1.-8]

B: an' that's not an awful lotta fruitcake.

    (1.0)

B: Course it is. A little piece goes a long way.

A: Well that's right.

(Continued)

(Continued)

The features associated with the production of agreements and disagreements also provide a framework within which disagreements can be upgraded. Since they provide resources for the avoidance and mitigation of overt conflict, speakers can strengthen their disagreements by declining to use them, that is by producing disagreements without any form of delay or mitigation, as in the case of C's disagreement with D in Extract 3.15.

> Extract 3.15 [G:II:2:33]
>
> D: If y'go ttuh Switzerland yer payin about fifty per cent a' yer money in ta:xes.
>
> C: Not in Switzerland
>
> D: (No) I think it i:s.

Within CA, differences between the structural features of the turns and sequences in which agreements and disagreements occur are described in terms of a 'preference organization' in which some actions are preferred (produced immediately and without mitigation) and their alternatives are 'dispreferred' (delayed and mitigated). In the case of agreeing and disagreeing with assessments, Pomerantz thus characterizes agreements as 'preferred actions' and disagreements as 'dispreferred actions' (Pomerantz, 1975, 1984).

Preference organization is a fundamental aspect of mundane conversation which operates in contexts in which agreement/disagreement becomes relevant. Although disagreements are dispreferred actions in most contexts, in some situations they are preferred actions. So, for example, Pomerantz (1975, 1978) shows that disagreement rather than agreement is the preferred activity in contexts in which it represents an affiliative as opposed to a disaffiliative action (e.g. following self-deprecations). Analysis of deviant cases confirms that participants in talk-in-interaction orient to these structural preferences.

Single Case Analysis

In a single case analysis, the researcher develops an analysis of a single episode of interaction, focusing on either a single interaction or a segment of a single interaction in order to track the interactional practices through which participants accomplish particular actions or activities (Schegloff, 1987a, 1987b). Single case analyses have been used by CA researchers to study institutional interactions that involve misunderstandings or other complications that have serious real world ramifications for the participants. This involves using the approach and findings of CA to further understanding of how these situations arise. As an example of a single case analysis, Box 3.2 provides a summary of a well-known CA study of a fateful call to an emergency service centre in the United States, which was conducted by Whalen et al. (1988).

Box 3.2   Single case analysis of a call to an emergency service centre

In this call to the emergency service centre, a caller reported that his stepmother was experiencing difficulty breathing and was dying. However, the call-takers (including a desk operator, a qualified nurse and her supervisor) did not immediately alert the relevant medical services, largely because the nurse dispatcher became embroiled in an argument with the caller. As a result of the medical services not being alerted, an ambulance was not dispatched even though the caller's stepmother was in fact seriously ill. Whalen et al. (1988) undertook a single case analysis of this seemingly aberrant event in order to understand how the call descended into an argument. They showed that this was due to a misalignment between the participants, which was not the fault of one person. In order to demonstrate this they began by distinguishing between two alternative forms of service transaction:

> Some service providers require little more than a request and an address, e.g., for the delivery of a pizza or the dispatch of a taxi: what we for convenience call a Type I service. For providers of Type I service, the need for the service (as opposed to the desire for it expressed in the request) is usually not an issue. In contrast, the existence of prima facia need for the service is a central consideration for what we call a Type II service, e.g., that provided by public agencies such as police and fire departments. The range of troubles that callers report to such agencies are in varying degrees screened for those which constitute problems for which providers must by policy or legal mandate take responsibility. (Whalen et al., 1988: 346)

Whalen et al. show that the caller requests an ambulance within a Type I frame – which establishes an expectation of the immediate dispatch of an ambulance – whereas the call taker(s) process the request within a Type II frame – which establishes the expectation of a pre-screening procedure at the outset of the call. This resulted in a fundamental misalignment between the participants concerning the 'ground rules' of the exchange that was unfolding. As can be seen in the following extract, this misalignment is evident from the outset of the call when the caller briefly speaks to a desk operator before asking to be transferred to a nurse.

(Continued)

(Continued)

> Extract 3.16
>
> | | |
> |---|---|
> | 1 Desk operator: | <u>Fire department.</u> |
> | 2 | (0.8) |
> | 3 Caller: | Yes, I'd like tuh have an ambulance at forty one thirty nine |
> | 4 | Haverford please |
> | 5 | (0.5) |
> | 6 Desk operator: | What's thuh <u>problem</u> sir? |
> | 7 Caller: | I: don't know, n'if I knew I wouldn't be <u>ca:</u>lling you all |
> | 8 | (0.5) |
> | 9 Desk operator: | Are <u>you</u> thuh one th't need th'ambulance? |
> | 10 Caller: | No I am not. It's my <u>mo</u>ther. |
> | 11 | (0.3) |
> | 12 Desk operator: | Lemme letya speak with thuh nurse |
> | 13 | (0.3) |
> | 14 Caller: | Oh bu:ll <u>shit!</u> |

Following the caller's request for an ambulance to be dispatched (lines 3-4), the desk operator initiated a pre-screening procedure by requesting details of the problem (line 6). This evokes a negative reaction from the caller, which implies that the desk operator's question was inappropriate, which it would be in the context of a Type I service encounter (line 7). Continuing to operate within the framework of a Type II service encounter, the desk operator subsequently pursues additional details/information by asking whether it is the caller who needs an ambulance (line 9). The caller answers by indicating that it is his mother who needs an ambulance (line 10). Once again, however, his response conveys his impatience and displeasure with the desk operator asking for additional information. It is at this point that the desk operator transfers the call to a nurse (line 12). The caller's subsequent expletive underlines his negative reaction to the trajectory of the call (line 14).

Whalen et al. go on to show how the call continues along similar lines when the caller speaks to the nurse and her supervisor and show how this underpins the descent of the call into an argument and ultimately to an ambulance not being dispatched even though the caller's mother was in fact very seriously ill (and subsequently passed away). Whalen et al. (1988: 358) conclude that:

> Our investigation revealed that the participants had rather different understandings of what was happening and different expectations of what was supposed to happen in this conversation. (...) This misalignment contributed in a fundamental way to a dispute that contaminated and transformed the participants' activity: the eliciting and giving of information concerning the condition of the caller's stepmother was displaced by the activity of arguing.

CONSTRAINTS ON ANALYSIS

Each utterance in talk-in-interaction is oriented to and displays some form of understanding of the utterance(s) that precede it, which may or may not be accepted by subsequent speakers. Analysis emerges from the orientations and understandings that parties routinely display to each other during their interactions. Consider the following example.

Extract 3.17 (SBL: 10: 12) (Source: Heritage, 1984)
B: Why don't you come and see me sometimes?
A: I would like to.
B: I would like you too.

Here Speaker B's initial utterance 'Why don't you come and see me sometimes?' is potentially open to a number of different interpretations. In principle, it could be treated as a question, a complaint or an invitation, amongst other actions. Notice, however, that the recipient (speaker A) treats B's utterance as an invitation by responding with an 'acceptance' (rather than, for example, an answer or an apology or excuse) and that speaker B confirms this interpretation ('I would like you too') rather than, for example, indicating that it was issued as a question or a complaint ('Yes but why don't you'). As Sacks et al. (1974: 729) observed, the availability of participants' publicly displayed analyses of each other's utterances means that:

> while understandings of other turns' talk are displayed to coparticipants, they are available as well to professional analysts who are thereby afforded a proof criterion (and search procedure) for the analysis of what a turn's talk is occupied with. Since it is the parties' understandings of prior turns' talk that is relevant to their construction of next turns, it is their understandings that are wanted for analysis. The display of those understandings in the talk of subsequent turns afford both a resource for the analysis of prior turns and a proof procedure for professional analyses of prior turns – resources intrinsic to the data themselves.

A fundamental constraint within CA is that analysis must remain grounded in these publicly displayed orientations and understandings, with attention being paid to whether they are ratified or not by co-participants in each successive turn at talk.

It should be emphasized that conversation analysts do not regard the orientations and understandings that participants display to each other as their interactions unfold as a window on participants' minds. These are *displayed* understandings that may or may not reflect or communicate what participants are actually thinking. So, for example, in the case of the utterance 'Why don't you come and see me sometimes' the second speaker may actually have interpreted the first speaker's utterance as a complaint, but nonetheless chose to treat it as an invitation. Moreover, the first speaker could either have actually intended the utterance to be heard as an invitation or, for one reason or another, decided to go along with this analysis, even though they produced the utterance as a complaint or a question or whatever. The understandings that participants display of each other's contributions may or may not represent what they are thinking. However, from the perspective of CA, these understandings provide a crucial resource when analysing the practices through which participants in talk-in-interaction produce, interpret and coordinate their social actions and social activities. This is because it is these understandings that participants have to manage, respond to and coordinate.

CA also places constraints on the use of 'wider' social and organizational roles and contexts to explain features of talk in interaction. Participants in talk-in-interaction can be accurately categorized in terms of numerous social identities, including those related to age, race, sex, social class, occupation and rank in an organizational setting (Sacks, 1992). This poses the question of how professional analysts can determine which, if any, of the array of social identities that can be applied to participants are relevant to understanding their conduct at any given point in time (Schegloff, 1991, 1992a, 1992b; see also Heritage and Clayman, 2010).

In response to this question, CA distinguishes between discourse identities, such as 'questioner–answerer' and 'inviter–invitee', which are intrinsic to talk-in-interaction and larger social and organizational identities (Goodwin, 1987), such as sex, ethnicity and occupational role, which derive from wider societal and institutional formations and thus reach beyond the talk itself. You will find that some CA studies restrict their focus to discourse identities, examining the sequentially organized aspects of talk-in-interaction which are relatively autonomous of other aspects of social organization. Pomerantz's analysis of agreements and disagreements with second assessments is an example of a study that adopts this approach.

However, other CA researchers do explore how participants make larger social and organizational identities relevant within their talk and how the invocation of such identities can constitute both a constraint on and a resource for the accomplishment of the activities in which the participants are engaged. In the case of ordinary conversation, for example, Goodwin (1987) shows how a speaker at a family gathering makes relevant his spousal relationship with a co-participant by producing a display of uncertainty about household affairs which positions the latter as a 'knowing recipient' and the other participants as 'unknowing recipients'. In the case of institutional talk, research on television and radio news interviews shows how discourse identities (and the activities in which they are embedded) invoke the institutional identities of participants in the UK and some other countries (including the USA) by positioning the broadcast journalists as formally neutral 'questioners', the guests as 'answerers', and the television or radio audience as 'primary recipients' of the talk (Clayman and

Heritage, 2002; Greatbatch, 1988; Heritage and Greatbatch, 1991). Thus, rather than viewing context as 'encompassing' social interaction, CA focuses on those aspects of context that can be shown to be relevant to the participants themselves as their interactions unfold.

ANALYSING TALK IN INSTITUTIONAL SETTINGS

As a student in business and management studies you will be studying some form of organizational talk (institutional talk in the CA parlance). The first point to note when applying CA in this way is that CA views ordinary conversation as the paramount and generic form of talk-in-interaction. Ordinary conversation represents a 'benchmark' against which other institutional forms of talk-in-interaction can be compared. CA research has shown that institutional forms of interaction, when compared with ordinary conversation, show systematic differences and restrictions on interactional activities and their design.

Harvey Sacks, Emanuel Schegloff and Gail Jefferson (1974) were the first to highlight the importance of this kind of comparative analysis. In their seminal article they note that turn-taking systems form a linear array in terms of the ways in which they operate to allocate turns at talk:

> The linear array is one in which one polar type (which conversation instances) involves 'one turn at a time allocation'; that is, the use of local allocational means, and the other pole (which debates instance) involves 'preallocation of all turns,' and medial types (which meetings instance) involve various mixes of preallocational and local allocational means. (Sacks et al., 1974: 729)

Sacks, Schegloff and Jefferson do not propose the independent status of conversation and ceremony as polar types. As noted above, ordinary conversation is considered the basic form of speech-exchange system, with other turn-taking systems representing transformations of the one used for ordinary conversation. In this light, debate or ceremony is not an independent polar type, but rather the most extreme transformation of ordinary conversation (Sacks et al., 1974: 729).

Building on these insights, Drew and Heritage (1992b) distinguish between interactions in 'formal settings' and 'non-formal settings'. Formal institutional interactions involve the use of specialized turn-taking systems which, in contrast to the turn-taking system for ordinary conversation, place strong constraints on such features as the order in which participants speak and the actions they undertake when they are allocated a turn at talk. These generally involve question–answer turn-taking formats used in the courtroom, various types of interview and some forms of pedagogic interaction. Think, for example, of a court in session in which lawyers are strictly restricted to asking questions and witnesses are restricted to answering them and are negatively sanctioned, usually by a judge, if they are deemed to depart from this arrangement. In formal settings, then, participants orient to the relevance of institutional contexts by attending to the constraints established by specialized turn-taking systems. This can have important implications for the ways in which various social activities are accomplished. So, for example, in courtroom interactions, counsel and witnesses often have to manage accusations and rebuttals in the form of questions and answers respectively (Atkinson and Drew, 1979). In the case of formal institutional talk then, CA researchers examine the ways in which specialized turn-taking systems are structured and how this informs the ways in which participants accomplish their roles.

Non-formal institutional interaction exhibits patterns of conduct that are less rigid or uniform than formal institutional interaction. Although non-formal institutional interaction may be characterized by aggregate asymmetries in the patterning of conduct between role incumbents, official tasks and activities are managed within turn-taking frameworks that allow for considerable variation, improvisation and negotiation as to the course the interaction will follow. Drew and Heritage (1992b: 28) observe that 'When considered in turn taking terms, at least, the boundaries between non-formal forms of institutional interaction and ordinary conversation can appear permeable and uncertain.' Non-formal interaction commonly occurs in medical, psychiatric, social service, business and related environments.

Drew and Heritage (1992b) suggest that, in contrast to formal institutional interaction, non-formal institutional interaction often does not exhibit specific recurrent interactional sequences, which are indicative of its institutional character. Therefore, researchers have to locate its institutional character:

> in a complex of non-recursive interactional practices that may vary in their form and frequency. Systematic aspects of the organization of sequences (and of turn design within sequences) having to do with such matters as the opening and closing of encounters, with the ways in which the information is requested, delivered, and received, with the design of referring expressions, etc are now beginning to emerge as facets of the ways in which the 'institutionality' of such encounters are managed. (Drew and Heritage, 1992b: 28)

CA stresses that the institutional character of both formal and non-formal institutional interaction is an interactional accomplishment, and is thus produced and confirmed by participants on a turn-by-turn basis rather than reflecting an established, antecedent structure. When people talk, they are simultaneously and reflexively talking their relationships, organizations and whole institutions into 'being' (Boden, 1994:14). Institutional structures, then, should be understood as the product of participants' actions rather than as 'containers' of those actions.

These insights into institutional interaction provide a firm foundation on which to build studies of talk in organizational settings. In terms of your research they provide an analytical framework that can be used to start noticing interesting phenomena in your data. One element to look for at the outset is similarities and differences between the ways in which social actions and activities are coordinated in your data as compared with ordinary conversation and perhaps other related settings.

It should be noted that when CA is used to study interaction in unfamiliar and in some cases complex organizational settings, CA researchers sometimes use interviews, informal discussions with staff, reviews of documentation, such as training manuals, and examination of software packages in order to understand the nature of the tasks and roles of the participants. So, for example, if you were studying calls to a telemedicine call line which uses a protocol-based computer triage system to establish whether callers should be directed to their General Practitioners or given emergency assistance or simply provided with advice as to how to deal with their condition themselves, you would need to understand the triage system in order to fully comprehend the contributions of the call taker. You might also need to understand the broader context in which the call takers operate, for example in terms of how their role relates to other roles, as well as to management structures. To gather this information it would be necessary to use other sources of information such as interviews, documentary analysis and observation. However, you would not use this information to explain what takes place in the recordings unless it can be shown to be relevant to the participants themselves in the course of the interactions.

CHAPTER SUMMARY

Within this chapter we have considered the following issues:

- Advantages and potential limitations of using audio and video recordings of naturally occurring interaction to study talk-in-interaction
- Identifying research questions through unmotivated reviews of recordings, reading other people's publications, or on the basis of practical concerns
- Developing and using transcriptions of recordings
- Analysing the sequential organization of social interaction, whilst eschewing a priori theorizing
- The distinction between CA studies that focus on the analysis of one particular recording (so-called single case analysis) and those that systematically compare episodes drawn from multiple recordings (so-called collection studies)
- Grounding empirical analyses and theoretical claims in the orientations and understandings that participants display to one another as their interactions unfold in real time
- Some aspects of the ways in which CA studies approach the analysis of talk in institutional settings, including a distinction that is made between formal and non-formal institutional interaction.

4

CONDUCTING RESEARCH USING CONVERSATION ANALYSIS

In this chapter, we provide a step-by-step guide to conducting a CA study. The design of a CA study is similar to that of many qualitative research designs and, as indicated in Chapter 3, includes the following features: formulating initial research questions, obtaining or making recordings of naturally occurring social interactions, transcribing data, using inductive analytic strategies and drawing out the theoretical contribution of the findings. In the sections that follow, we discuss the specific steps involved in CA research; however, it is important to remember that in practice CA studies are often iterative, involving researchers moving back and forth between the stages we describe as new findings and observations emerge.

STEPS INVOLVED IN CA RESEARCH

As indicated in Chapter 1, our description of the steps involved in a CA study is organized around the steps shown in Box 4.1.

Box 4.1   Steps in Conversation Analysis

Data collection

↓

Formulation of research questions

↓

Transcription of data

↓

Data analysis

↓

Identification of contribution to knowledge

↓

Writing up findings

Step 1: Data Collection

As noted in Chapter 1, you can obtain data for your CA study in four main ways.

1. You can set up your own audio or video recording equipment in order to record face-to-face or technologically mediated interactions, including telephone calls, video calls and web-based conversations.
2. You can acquire access to recordings made by other people; for example, many organizations record inbound and/or outbound calls to their call centres for quality assurance and training purposes.
3. You can record radio or television programmes.
4. You can download recordings from a number of sites on the Internet, including YouTube, Metacafe and TED Talks.

Before you start your study, you need to be certain that your data is appropriate for a CA study. The questions you need to answer are as follows:

1. Does your data comprise audio or video recordings of naturally occurring interaction?
2. Is the quality good enough for you to focus on the fine details of the interaction?
3. Is your data suitable for a study in the field of business and management research? Was it collected in an organizational setting or does it involve relevant issues being discussed?

Once you have satisfied yourself that your data are suitable for a CA study in the field of business and management research, you should ensure that:

1. You have informed consent from the participants to use the data in your proposed research study.
2. You have informed consent for use of the data in your proposed study from any other stakeholders, such as the organizations that have provided you with recordings or permitted you to collect recordings.

If your data has been recorded from the broadcast media or was downloaded from the web, consider whether there are any ethical or copyright issues that need to be addressed.

Step 2: Formulation of Research Questions

The first step in CA is to familiarize yourself with your audio or video recordings and identify and/or refine your research questions. As noted in Chapter 2, Sacks (1992) suggested that research questions should emerge from unmotivated looking while reviewing audio or video recordings, rather than be formulated a priori. This involves a data-driven process in which the phenomena of interest and research questions emerge from an analyst reviewing recordings rather than being preselected on the basis of the analyst's research interests. Most CA researchers follow the path recommended by Sacks, or at least claim to do so. Of course, you may already know what you are interested in or have some preliminary questions based on personal experience or reading the literature concerning a particular topic. If so, you will start your study with a more or less clear idea of your research questions, although you should be prepared to refine these questions as you review your data.

Step 3: Transcription of Data

You now need to decide what you are going to transcribe. If you are undertaking a single case analysis then you will need to transcribe the interaction or stretch of interaction that contains the case you are interested in. If you are going to look at a collection of cases of a particular phenomenon, then you will need to identify where the cases are located on the audio or video recording ready for transcription.

You are now ready to transcribe your data, using the system developed by Gail Jefferson (2004). This stage (transcription) could well overlap with the previous stage (identifying research questions) and the next stage (data analysis). This is because as you transcribe your data it is possible that you will refine or even change your research questions as you become increasingly familiar with your data and, as you transcribe, you will inevitably start to analyse your data, noting candidate patterns of interactions and similarities and differences in the ways in which things are done.

It is possible to transcribe recordings of audio or video recordings using an ordinary media player. However, you can reduce the time required to transcribe recordings by up to a half by using a foot pedal designed to connect to a computer to control the playback of digital recordings. Having installed digital foot pedal transcription software on your computer you can use the foot pedal to pause, rewind and fast forward a recording while continuing to use your keyboard to type, modify and format transcripts. Generally, you have a choice of transcribing directly into a file within a word processing programme (e.g. MS Word) or the transcription software that comes with the pedal. Transcription software may also offer valuable features for file management. Box 4.2 offers some tips that you may find helpful if you decide to purchase transcription equipment (although, of course, it may be possible to use equipment available at your host institution).

Box 4.2   Tips for using a transcription foot pedal and software

- Although you can buy transcription kits, it is generally cheaper to obtain a foot pedal and transcription software separately. Alternatively, ask whether the kit is supplied free at your institution.
- Check that the foot pedal is compatible with the file formats you are using (e.g. .mp3,.wav) and your computer's operating system.
- Free-to-download transcription software is widely available. Try out some of these free alternatives and choose the one that best meets your needs and compatibilities.
- Use a typist's headset or headphones that enclose your ears as they will reduce background noise and distractions.

A good way to start is by developing rough transcripts, laying out what each of the participants says without worrying about capturing all the details of their conduct. These transcripts will look something like this:

Extract 4.1a
1. R: ok can we just clarify one or two points
2.   ok
3. A: yes
4. R: you did a capstan setting operating course
5. A: yes I did yes
6. R: was was that a skills centre course
7. A: yes

You can then further develop the transcripts by using the CA transcription notation to identify overlaps and silences, as in Extract 4.1b:

Extract 4.1b
1. R: ok (0.2) can we just clarify one or two points
2.   (0.5)
3. R: ok
4. A: yes
5. R: you did a capstan setting operating course
6. A: yes [I did. Yes.
7. R: [was-
8. R: was that a skills centre [course
9. A: [yes

You will have noticed that in Extract 4.1b we have added timed silences of two-tenths of a second (0.2) and half a second (0.5) at lines 1 and line 2 respectively, and you may now be wondering how the lengths of silences are calculated. In answer to this question, there are three methods of timing silences, which can be summarized as follows:

• Using a stop watch and making repeated timings until you are sure you are catching the exact onset and end points of silences (Jefferson, 1989; Hepburn and Bolden, 2012; ten Have, 1999)
• Using computer-aided methods which allow researchers to read the acoustic pause length from a computer screen (Couper-Kuhlen, 2012; Hepburn and Bolden, 2012; Stivers, et al., 2009)
• Using 'speech rhythm-sensitive timing' which allows researchers to measure and understand silences relative to the pace of the talk that precedes them (Hepburn and Bolden, 2012; ten Have, 1999). To time silences in this way, researchers become accustomed to the tempo of the talk leading up to a silence and, as the silence begins, start counting at the pace of the preceding talk (Hepburn and Bolden, 2012; Wilson and Zimmerman, 1986). Generally speaking, when doing this researchers follow Gail Jefferson (1989) by using a method used by photographers

who count 'none one thousand, one one thousand, two one thousand' and so on to calculate timings to the nearest tenth of a second: a silence ending immediately following 'none' is recorded as a 0.2 second silence; a silence that ends after 'none one' is recorded as a 0.5 second silence; a silence that ends at 'none one thou-' is recorded as a 0.7 second; a silence that ends at 'none one thousand' is recorded as a one second silence, and so on. If a noticeable silence is shorter than 'none' (two-tenths of a second) it is recorded as a micro silence, which is represented in transcripts by a period in parenthesis (Hepburn and Bolden, 2012). This method was used to time the silences in Extract 4.1b.

Once you have added overlaps and silences to your transcripts, the next step is to look more closely at the sequencing of the interaction, the characteristics of speech delivery and, if you are analysing video recordings, nonverbal conduct. This requires familiarity with the CA transcription conventions, which are summarized in Box 4.3.

Box 4.3   CA transcription conventions

1. OVERLAPPING UTTERANCES: A left-hand bracket indicates the point at which overlapping talk begins, while a right-hand bracket indicates the point at which overlapping talk ends.

   M: Was this on the Monday?

   H: No that [was (in the following) week. The] Thursday.

   W: [No this was in the week. In the week.]

2. CONTIGUOUS UTTERANCES: When there is no gap between adjacent utterances, the utterances are linked together with an equals sign.

   H: I explained that as well. I'm not going into it. I'm sorry.=

   M: =Right.

3. PAUSES AND GAPS BETWEEN UTTERANCES: Numbers in parentheses indicate the lengths of silences in tenths of a second.

   H: But you've actually put the barriers up.

        (0.5)

   W: All ri:ght it's how you see it.= But I don't consider that I ha:ve

(Continued)

(Continued)

M: Uh::m (1.2) one of the things (0.2) I guess that one of the things the children (0.2) enjoy and need. hhh and base their lives on is quite a fir:m structure and routine.

A dot in parentheses (.) indicates a gap of less than two tenths of a second:

H: Is it possible to get a copy of it.

(.)

M: No it's only just for us.

4. CHARACTERISTICS OF SPEECH DELIVERY: Punctuation marks are used to capture characteristics of speech delivery – the way in which words are pronounced – rather than to mark conventional grammatical units. For example, a colon indicates an extension of the immediately preceding sound.

D: What happe:ned to him,

and additional colons are used to convey that a sound is stretched over a longer period:

N: Oh right you're right near Safe[way are you.

C: [O:::h yes and she regularly goes there.

Periods, commas and question marks are used respectively to indicate falling, slightly rising (non-terminal) and strongly rising intonation contours.

A: I was involved in a meeting.

M: Can't you include them in what you're doing on Sunday morning,

(.)

M: Is that possible?

A variety of symbols are used to indicate other aspects of speech delivery. A single dash indicates a cut-off sound like a guttural stop.

M: What [Doris is saying is that=

H: [It's- it's-

H: =It's under Doris's ter:ms all the ti:me.=

An upward pointing arrow indicates a marked rise in pitch, while a downward pointing arrow indicates a marked lowering of pitch.

Dr: I think you will ↓be fine (0.2) going on (.) ↑holiday next mon↓th

Underlining is used to indicate emphasis.

H: Yeah. ·hh The <u>kids</u> like to go in the club on a Sunday lunchti:me

Capital letters are used to indicate talk that is spoken louder than the surrounding talk.

H: you keep <u>saying</u> this (.) and I'm- I'm <u>still</u>

W: I KNOW BUT IT JUST SEEMED SO: well <u>ti</u>:::med.

H: Yeah.

A degree sign is used to indicate that part of an utterance is softer than the surrounding talk.

M: .hhh (.) I wonder how tha:t could have °happened° to him

Audible inhalations are represented by 'h's preceded by a period.

IR: .hhh Wouldn't the ide:al situation Jill be: that we ha:ve more national

he[alth=ser:vice clinics?

IE1:   [Oh Cer::tainly.

Audible aspirations are represented by hs without a preceding period.

W: hhhhh Well we're looking at thi:s (.) at the moment from Lester's point of view

H: No we're not,

Double parentheses contain descriptions by transcribers:

D: ((whispered)) Where is he?

D: That's a great idea:.

((Telephone rings))

B: That's probably Bob calling now.

'Greater than' and 'less than' signs are used to enclose a part of the utterance that is speeded up.

S: The Guar:dian <u>new</u>spaper l<u>oo</u>ked through>the manifestoes<las:st ↑week

5. TRANSCRIPTION DOUBT: Parenthesized words indicate that the transcriber was not sure of what was said and empty parenthesis indicates that the transcriber could not hear what was said.

(Continued)

(Continued)

W: You'd found out the evening before why didn't you ring us that evening

(and let us know) [( ).

H: [Because I don't have to

6. NON-VERBAL COMMUNICATION: CA researchers represent visual aspects of communication in a variety of ways. In our own research, we generally describe the participants' visual conduct in double parenthesis using brackets to indicate the position of the conduct in relation to the participants' talk.

Example 1

H: Yeah I'd like to see them every week?

M: [Y o u ' d l i k e t o y o u s e e t h e m e v e r y w e e k]

[((W mouths the word "no", shakes her head and gazes at the floor))]

H: [Yeah

[(W continues to shake her head and gaze at the floor))

Example 2

H: It was a Sunday I am by law by the Court order I- I have [access. I: should

[((W gazes at H))

[have access to Harriet every time.

[(W gazes at M)

M: [Mhm

[((As W gazes at M, she opens and closes her mouth))

H: Now she says says [Harriet isn't happy

[(W gestures with her hand, then looks away from M))

Heath et al.'s (2010) introduction to the use of video in qualitative research includes a useful glossary of transcription symbols that can be used to capture the fine-grained details of visual conduct in research that is informed by conversation analysis and ethnomethodology.

In order to familiarize yourself with the CA transcription symbols, we suggest you take some time to read transcripts from CA books and papers (see examples in Chapter 5 and the references below).

For a comprehensive list of the transcription symbols available for use in CA studies, see the glossary in Atkinson and Heritage's seminal collection of CA studies (1984: ix-xvi). You should also consider reading Hepburn and Bolden's (2012) very helpful discussion of the key CA transcription conventions, as they explain the importance of using the conventions, explore challenges for transcription and address criticisms that have been made about the CA approach to transcribing recordings of naturally occurring talk-in-interaction.

Once you have further developed your transcripts, using the CA transcription conventions, they will now look something like this:

Extract 4.1c
1. R: Ok (0.2) can we just cla- clarify one or two points,
2.   (0.5)
3. R: Ok?
4. A: yes
5. R: you did a capstan setting operating course::
6. A: yes [I did. Yea:h,
7. R: [was-
8. R: was that a- a skills centre [course?
9. A: [yes

Some CA transcriptions deviate from standard spellings of some words by using phoneticized spellings that are designed to capture the ways in which words are actually pronounced/articulated. For example, 'dju' for 'do you' and 'dz' for 'does'. We would suggest that you only do this if you can show that this is relevant to the interactional phenomenon that you are analysing – as would be the case, for example, if there was an apparent misunderstanding deriving from the ways in which words are pronounced.

It is important to note that when transcribing you will inevitably be analysing your data, identifying patterns and the like. Moreover, when undertaking analysis with advanced transcripts you may well refine your transcripts. So this phase should be treated as overlapping with data analysis and you should start to make analytic notes and observations, relating to individual cases and perhaps possible patterns of turn design and sequence organization.

Normally, transcriptions must be anonymized. You can replace the names of people, organizations and places with fictional alternatives, using your word processing software's search and replace facility. However, you will also need to read your transcripts very carefully in order to identify and amend passages that might compromise participants' anonymity (e.g. due to references to a proprietary product, a specific location, and so forth).

Box 4.4 provides some tips for transcribing talk-in-interaction, using the CA system.

Box 4.4   Tips for transcription

- Start out by examining transcripts in journal articles, book chapters and books. Note how researchers contextualize and lay out the transcripts, and how they identify features in them by reference to line arrows and line numbers.
- Use headings for your transcripts that: indicate their source and/or date of collection; remind you about their content; and enable you to readily locate the relevant audio or video recordings as and when required.
- Use a non-proportional font (also called fixed-pitch, fixed-width, or monospaced font), such as Courier or Courier New. In these fonts letters and characters each occupy the same amount of horizontal space and this makes it easier to align simultaneous speech as precisely as possible. With proportional fonts (such as Arial, Times New Roman and Verdana) letters and characters have different widths – e.g. the horizontal space used for the letter 'l' is less wide than that used for the letter 'w' – and this can make it difficult to align simultaneous talk.
- Remember that MS Word has a function for inserting line numbers. To add line numbers to your transcriptions in MS Word you:

  1. Put a continuous section break before and after your extract (use the Insert>Break menu).
  2. Click where you want the line numbering to begin.
  3. Go onto line numbers on Page Setup: File> PageSetup>Layout> Line numbers.
  4. Tick the Add Line Numbering box, and then select 'Restart Each Section'.

- Anonymize your data at an early stage, ideally directly after transcription. This will reduce the likelihood of you missing anything. Remember also that replacing real names with fictitious names might change the line numbering of your transcripts and that this could create quite a lot of unnecessary editing work for you if you had already started to develop and write up analyses of your transcripts using the original line numbers before anonymizing your data.
- Make sure that you keep back-up copies of your transcripts (and recordings).

To develop a more complete understanding, useful references for CA transcription include Atkinson and Heritage (1984), Hepburn and Bolden (2013) and Jefferson (2004).

Step 4: Data Analysis

Once you have developed your transcripts, the next stage is to work systematically through your data in order to address your research question(s). This entails you analysing the single case or collection of particular types of sequences that you have identified. If you are analysing a collection of examples of a phenomenon in which you are interested (e.g. sequences involving requests, complaints, disagreements), as opposed to a single case (e.g. a telephone call to a customer services centre that didn't go according to plan), your analysis will have two core phases. In the first phase, you identify and describe a candidate pattern in the way in which participants accomplish and coordinate their actions by analysing your examples on a case by case basis. Your description of phenomena will be both formal and situated. As Mazeland (2006: 159) notes: 'A description is formal when it is formulated at a level of generality that allows for a characterization of the recognizability of a device across contexts. A description is situated when the context is specified.'

Once you have identified a pattern of interaction, in a second phase you move on to establish whether the participants observably orient to this pattern. As noted in Chapter 3, this involves using the procedure known as deviant case analysis (Schegloff, 1968), whereby the conversation analyst examines cases in which participants depart from a described pattern and establish whether departures are treated as accountable by participants. As noted on page 27, this enables the analyst to ascertain whether the described pattern is an empirical regularity that occurs by happenstance, or whether the participants orient to the pattern as a normative interactional procedure (Heritage, 1995). Having examined deviant cases you will either conclude that the cases validate the basic pattern or, if they do not do this, modify the theory you have developed so far in order to accommodate the deviant cases. Usually, Phases 1 and 2 are repeated recursively. Your objective should be to develop an exhaustive description that accounts for all instances of the phenomenon of interest in your corpus of data.

If you use quantification to count the occurrence of your observed pattern(s), you must ensure that this only follows detailed analysis of the individual cases that are being quantified, with categories for quantification emerging from this analysis of individual cases. You should also remember that your quantitative analysis is subsidiary to qualitative exploration of the phenomenon in phase 1 and to qualitative validation of the candidate analysis in phase 2. Even if you use quantification, you still have to provide qualitative evidence that participants orient themselves to the pattern you have identified and give a plausible account of how they do this.

Single case analyses can be used to show how the results of collection studies in other settings do not necessarily apply in a particular instance, or to explore how particular outcomes (e.g. an argument or a premature termination of a telephone call) emerged and why.

Regardless of whether you focus on a single case or collections of cases, you should avoid trying to ascribe motivations to any particular action. You should focus on what the participants say and do, rather than trying to account for their actions in terms of their inner feelings and motivations. The only time you should focus on participants' 'inner' emotions or thoughts is when they refer to them in their interactions and, in that case, you should carefully avoid assessing whether their descriptions are accurate.

Step 5: Identification of Contribution to Knowledge

You must now locate your findings in relation to the literature related to your topic of investigation. This will enable you to clearly establish how the knowledge your research project has generated contributes to one or more research fields in the area of business and management. You could also consider how it contributes to CA studies of institutional interaction.

Step 6: Writing Up Findings

You now write up your findings in your dissertation, using extracts from transcripts of the audio or video recording(s) you have analysed as examples of the phenomena you describe. Your write-up should contain the following information:

- A statement of your research issues and questions and why they are of interest and important
- A description of your data collection strategies, the nature of your data, the participants, and your procedures for ensuring participant anonymity, and how you selected your extracts/examples
- A justification of your study design (single case/collection; verbal/nonverbal etc.)
- A systematic description of patterns of interaction found based on thorough data analysis, including examples
- Interpretations of how these patterns are embedded across all contexts in which they are found
- A discussion of how the findings shed light on theoretical and practical issues in business and management research.

In the next section we illustrate the CA approach by reference to one of our CA studies, which investigated the dissemination of management ideas on the international management lecture circuit.

CASE STUDY: MANAGEMENT GURU LECTURES[1]

Step 1: Data Collection

The data for our study comprised video recordings of the public lectures of an elite group of management thought leaders, who are often referred to as management gurus (see Greatbatch and Clark, 2003, 2005, 2010). Management gurus are purveyors of influential management ideas such as Excellence, Culture Change, Learning Organization, and Business Process Reengineering. In addition to writing best-selling management books they disseminate their ideas in live presentations across the world on the international management lecture circuit (Huczynski, 1993; Jackson, 2001). As perhaps amongst the highest-profile group of management speakers in the world, they use their lectures to build their personal reputations with audiences of managers. Many gain reputations as powerful orators and subsequently market recordings of their talks as parts of audio, video-and web-based management training packages often marketed by their own eponymous organizations.

The video recordings were drawn from commercially produced training packages, most of which were provided free of charge by training companies that we approached and who were interested in our research. The videos analysed in the study featured Daniel Goleman, Rosabeth Moss Kanter, Gary Hamel, Tom Peters and Peter Senge. The 20 hours of video material contained approximately 15 hours of the gurus lecturing to audiences of managers.

Step 2: Formulation of Research Questions

Initial viewings of the recordings revealed that the lectures are not episodes of one-way communication in which the speaker sends a message and the audience passively receive it. Rather, members of the audience actively participate in the proceedings. While the lectures do not contain any disaffiliative responses such as booing and heckling, audience members do regularly produce displays of affiliation with the gurus by, inter alia, clapping, laughing supportively, nodding their heads and smiling. In some cases, these affiliative responses are produced by one or two individuals. In others, however, they involve numerous audience members acting in concert with each other. When audience members collectively display their affiliation with the gurus, they do so predominantly by laughing in response to purportedly humorous messages. In the light of these observations, we formulated the following research questions:

---

[1]This section draws from and reproduces material from Greatbatch and Clark (2003), which is used by permission of SAGE Publications.

- How is audience laughter evoked and coordinated?
- What is the relationship between the humour, laughter and the gurus' core ideas?

Step 3: Transcription of Data

We identified 88 cases of collective audience laughter and decided that we had suf-ficient time and resources to transcribe all of these episodes of laughter and the surrounding talk. We then transcribed the data, using transcription symbols drawn from the CA transcription notation and additional symbols devised by Max Atkinson in his CA studies of political oratory (for details on this notation see Atkinson and Heritage, 1984; Greatbatch and Clark, 2003, 2005). These symbols enabled us to develop transcripts which captured fine-grained details of the delivery of the seg-ments of the lectures which gave rise to laughter, the positioning of audience laughter in relation to these messages and the timing and delivery of the gurus' subsequent talk. While transcribing the data, we began to analyse the data, starting out by addressing the first of our research questions.

Step 4: Data Analysis

We analysed the data in terms of our two key research questions, first identifying pat-terns of interaction and then using deviant case analysis to establish whether these patterns were oriented to by the speakers and audience members.

Research Question 1: How is laughter evoked and coordinated?

Phase 1: Identifying patterns of interaction

By repeatedly viewing and analysing the cases of collective audience laughter and refining the transcripts as we did so, we identified two interrelated patterns of con-duct. The first concerns the timing and coordination of episodes of audience laughter and builds on the findings of previous CA studies of public speaking (largely political oratory) (e.g. Atkinson 1984a, 1984b; Clayman, 1993; Heritage and Greatbatch, 1986). According to Clayman (1992, 1993), collective audience responses, such as applause and laughter, may be facilitated by two methods: independent decision-making and mutual monitoring. Independent decision-making involves audience members react-ing independently of one another but nonetheless managing to respond in concert. In this respect audience members gravitate to those parts of a speech that stand out conspicuously from other parts of the talk. Where audience members can anticipate the completion of such a message, then 'its completion may serve as a common refer-ence point around which independent response decisions are coordinated' (Clayman,

1993: 112). In contrast, mutual monitoring involves 'response decisions being guided, at least in part, by reference to the [aural or less commonly visual] behaviour of other audience members' (Clayman, 1993: 112). Thus, for example, individual audience members may decide to respond after they observe others doing likewise or acting in ways which suggest that they are about to do so (e.g. preparing to clap, murmuring approval and nodding). As Clayman (1993) notes, these two scenarios lead to different types of responses. Responses that are mainly facilitated by independent decision-making begin with a 'burst' and quickly grow in intensity as numerous audience members respond in concert. The ability of individual audience members to respond in concert at or near to message completion points depends upon speakers supplying their messages with emphasis and clearly projectable completion points around which audience members can coordinate their actions. Responses that are primarily organized by mutual monitoring are characterized by 'staggered' onsets as involving the reactions of a handful of audience members. Our review of the guru lectures suggested that independent decision-making plays a predominant role in the genesis of collective audience laughter in the lectures, as all but 5 of the 88 episodes of audience laughter begin with a burst, either just before or immediately after message completion.

The second pattern of conduct we identified was that, in most cases, audience laughter is not simply a spontaneous reaction to messages whose content is self-evidently humorous. Usually audience laughter is 'invited' by the gurus through the use of a range of verbal and nonverbal practices, which establish the relevance of audience laughter. Thus the gurus 'highlight' their messages in relation to surrounding speech through volume, pitch or stress variation; marked speeding up or other rhythmic shifts; and/or facial, hand and/or body gestures. They also supply the messages with clearly projectable completion points, around which audience members can coordinate their responses. Moreover, rather than relying on audience members to recognize their humorous intent from the content of their messages alone, they establish the relevance of audience laughter by, for example, (1) announcing that they are about to say something humorous, (2) smiling or laughing and/or (3) using 'comedic' facial expressions, gestures and prosody – including, for example, displays of emotions such as disgust, disbelief, anger, horror and amazement by themselves or others to the actions, practices or issues that are being discussed. This is not to say that these nonverbal actions are inherently 'comedic'. Their possible status as such derives from their use with particular verbal messages and devices, whose 'comedic' status in turn derives in part from their use with such nonverbal actions. In other words, the speakers' verbal and nonverbal actions are reflexively related – the comedic status of each resting in part on their use in conjunction with the other.

The following data extract from a speech by Tom Peters contains relatively straightforward examples of both these phenomena and the level of detail involved in our research. In this extract, Peters supports his argument that organizations should adopt 'flat and fluid' structures by quoting Ross Perot. The quotation praises one company, Electronic Data Systems (EDS), for purportedly adopting a 'flat and fluid' structure, and disparages another company, General Motors (GM), for purportedly retaining a cumbersome bureaucratic structure. Both the commendation of EDS and the criticism of GM are followed by audience laughter.

Extract 4.2

```
 1  TP:          My favourite Perroism of all was his description, right before
 2               leaving GM, of what he sa:w as the difference between
 3               Electronic Data Systems and GM. (0.6) He said,
 4               ['At EDS (.) WHEN YOU SEE A SNAKE (.) YOU KILL IT'.
 5               [Leans forward, glares, uses angry tone of voice
 6  Audience:->  [LLLLLLLLLL LLLLLLLLLL LLLLLL-L-L[-L
 7               [Turns and walks                          [
 8  Peters:                                           [He said, 'At GM when
 9               you see a snake, [you search the world for the top
10                               [Leans forward/smile face
11               consultant on snakes'.
12  Audience:->  LLLLLLLLLL LLLLLLLLLL
13  Peters:      Then you appoint a committee on snakes and you study
14               snakes for the next two years. (1.0) <Flat (.) fluid (.) and get
                 on with it (.) that':s the creature
```

Peters provides the messages that evoke laughter with both emphasis and clearly projectable completion points by, inter alia, using a puzzle-solution format (Atkinson, 1984a, 1984b; Heritage and Greatbatch, 1986). Thus he begins by establishing a puzzle in the minds of the audience members (lines 1-3): what did Ross Perot see as the difference between EDS and GM? He then offers a two-part solution which is formed as a contrast (lines 3-4 and 8-9 and 11). In this way, he highlights the contents of the messages against a background of surrounding speech materials. He also provides the audience members with resources to anticipate the completion of the two messages, for they can match each part of the emerging solution to the puzzle in order to infer what it will take for it to be complete. In the case of the second part of the solution/contrast, they can also match it against the first part. In both instances, Peters confirms the relevance of laughter by ceding the floor until the audience's laughter ends (lines 6 and 12) and then, when he resumes speaking, neither asserting nor otherwise indicating that the audience's laughter was inappropriate or unexpected (lines 13-15).

Peters does not solely rely on the 'humorous' content of his remarks to establish the relevance of audience laughter; he also 'invites' audience laughter by using a range of nonverbal techniques. In the first case of laughter (line 6), which follows Peters's depiction of Perot's commendation of EDS, Peters uses comedic gestures, facial expressions and prosody. As he quotes Perot on EDS, he suddenly leans forward, glares at a section of the audience and speaks louder as he adopts a 'mock angry' tone (lines 4-5). Then, as he completes the quotation ('you kill it'), he bares his teeth as he 'spits' out the words. Together with Perot's incongruous metaphorical imagery - seeing and killing snakes in a corporate context - Peters' nonverbal actions establish the possible relevance of audience laughter. In the second case of audience laughter (line 12), which follows Peters' depiction of Perot's disparagement of GM (lines 8-9 and 11), Peters, reverting to a 'low key' form of speech delivery, establishes the possible relevance of laughter by leaning forward and smiling at the audience as he completes the quotation (line 10). Thus, Peters does not solely rely on the content of his message to indicate to audience members that his message is humorous and that laughter is an appropriate response.

Phase 2: Deviant Case Analysis

The next stage was to review the handful of deviant/incongruous cases in which the practices illustrated in this extract were absent. This served to confirm our thesis that the projection of clear message completion points and the signalling of humorous intent are key to understanding the evocation of collective audience laughter. For example, the importance of signalling humorous intent to audience members is underscored by the fact that in all but one of the five laughter episodes in which the onset of audience laughter is 'staggered' (i.e. it does not begin within an immediate 'burst') the gurus rely on audience members to recognize on the basis of the content of their messages alone that laughter is a relevant, if not an expected response. Consider Extract 4.3 in which Rosabeth Moss Kanter evokes audience laughter after she describes the purported reactions of a number of giant American corporations to a new packaging technology. After Kanter's description one or two audience members start to laugh.

Extract 4.3 [GCBA1: 00.21.15]

```
1   RMK:   They were the first producer of fruit and vegetable juice in the
2          United States (.) to put their product in the cute little paper
3          bottle.=The ( ) packaging. (0.7) A well known packaging
4          technology all over Europe not used in the United States. I mean
5          again it just shows we're scouting the world (0.5) for technology
6          including things like packaging can make a huge difference. (.)
```

```
 7              Anyhow they were not known in the United States. In the early
 8              eighties the European manufacturers came over (.) to make
 9              presentations to (0.2) to all the food companies to see if they could
10              interest them in the packaging. (.) So they make presentations to
11              all of the giants, Coca Cola, (.) Proctor and Gamble etcetera and
12              one of the gia:nts (0.5) was sufficiently interested in this that they
13              immediately set up a committee to study it.
14              (.)
15   Aud:   L-L[-L-L -L- L- L- L      [LLLLLL-L-L-L- [L
16              [Expansive smile [                            [
17   RMK:                    [Right (.) uhm    [
18   RMK:                                        [Ocean Spra::y heard
19              the same presentation (0.8) committed the next da:y, (0.5) signed a
20              deal by the end of the week, (0.4) and got an eighteen month
21              exclusive license.
```

The absence of an immediate burst of laughter may index, in part, uncertainty on the part of audience members as to whether collective laughter is relevant at this particular juncture. Kanter presents her message in a relatively straightforward way, with the result that the potential relevance of laughter rests largely, if not solely, on the content of her remarks. Subsequently, Kanter confirms that laughter is relevant by not only falling silent, but also smiling (line 16). However, the audience members' audible response remains limited to isolated laughter (line 15). In the face of this, Kanter stops smiling and, walking away from the audience, resumes speaking (line 17: 'Right'). As she does so, however, additional audience members start to laugh – possibly in response not only to the preceding isolated laughter, but also to Kanter's expansive smile. Kanter hesitates momentarily and then, as the laughter dissolves, goes on to praise the actions of a smaller company called Ocean Spray which, she claims, is not weighed down by bureaucracy (line 18–21). Examples like this perhaps underline the importance of the cues that gurus routinely use to signal their humorous intent to audience members.

In summary, we found that collective audience laughter is not simply a spontaneous reaction to messages whose content is self-evidently humorous. Usually, audience laughter is 'invited' by the gurus through the use of a range of verbal and nonverbal practices, which supply their messages with emphasis and clearly projected turn completion points and signal humorous intent.

Having identified a number of generic techniques through which audience laughter is invited and coordinated during the gurus' lectures, we turned to consider the relationship between the messages which evoke audience laughter and the gurus' core ideas and visions. Once again we used the standard two-phase CA approach of identifying patterns and then considering deviant cases.

Research Question 2: What is the relationship between humour, laughter and the gurus' core ideas?

Phase 1: Identifying patterns of interaction

Working through the transcripts on a case by case basis, we found that there were only three cases in which the gurus offered audience members opportunities to express through laughter unvarnished expressions of support for the values that are embedded in their core ideas and visions. In all of the other cases messages which precipitate laughter are constructed in ways which mean that subsequent audience laughter is not open to interpretation as unequivocal and unvarnished expressions of support for the management gurus' core ideas. This is because the gurus invest their messages with multiple sources of humour and/or invite displays of affiliation with values that do not derive directly from their core management ideas and visions. This enables the gurus to elicit collective displays of affiliation, regardless of whether audience members agree with their core ideas and visions. Thus, for example, if you look again at Extract 4.2 you will see that this is the case when Tom Peters quotes Ross Perot. Here Peters evokes laughter in response to his (and Perot's) praise of the supposedly rapid reaction of one organization, and criticism of the purportedly slow reactions of another. In so doing, Peters conveys a critique of big, 'bureaucratic' organizations. However, there are several other potential sources of humour, including Perot's metaphorical imagery and style of speaking, and Peters' mimicry of these. Consequently, individual audience members may be displaying their appreciation of the humour in these features, as opposed to (or in addition to) Perot's evaluation of the corporations' actions and, by extension, Peters' core ideas. This means that while audience members engage in collective displays of affiliation with Peters, their laughter does not represent unvarnished expressions of support for the position he is using the Perot quotation to substantiate.

Phase 2: Deviant case analysis

Next we turned to consider the three deviant/incongruous cases in which the gurus seem to invite audience members to express – through laughter – unvarnished support for values that are embodied in their core management ideas and visions. One of these cases is provided in Extract 4.3 above in which, as we have seen, Kanter evokes laughter in response to her depiction of the reactions of large corporations to an innovative packaging technology. To a large extent appreciation of the humour of her remarks, which are produced 'straight-faced', derives from acceptance of her espoused view that most large organizations are too cautious when they encounter innovatory practices and products. Consequently, the audience's laughter is open to interpretation as an unvarnished expression of support for her ideas concerning organizational practice in general.

Our analysis of deviant cases enabled us to develop a clear *technical* distinction between cases in which audience laughter represents unvarnished displays of affiliation with the speakers' core ideas and visions and those in which they do not. This enabled us to ensure that our analysis was systematic - rather than impressionistic - and grounded in the details of the interaction. Of course, this left open the question of what the implications of the use/non-use of the practices we identified might be. While we could not answer this through our analysis, we did offer some thoughts/ suggestions, which could be explored in future CA research. In brief, we suggested that the fact that the gurus routinely 'play safe' by inviting audience laughter which is not open to interpretation as an unvarnished expression of support for their core positions is perhaps not surprising. The gurus often recommend practices that audience members are unlikely to be using and criticize practices that audience members are likely to be using. Although managers may welcome exposure to ideas that question what they do, it does not follow that they will wish to affiliate publicly with them. By inviting audience laughter which is not open to interpretation as an unvarnished expression of support for their core ideas, the gurus may, amongst other things, increase their chances of generating affiliative exchanges with audience members, even if these conditions apply.

Step 5: Identification of Contribution to Knowledge

Having completed the analysis we then moved on to consider how our findings contributed to business and management research. We argued that our research offered a distinctive perspective on two interrelated issues which have attracted widespread attention in business and management research, namely humour and group cohesiveness. Previous research into the functions of humour suggest that it can promote the emergence and maintenance of group cohesiveness by, inter alia, clarifying and reinforcing shared values and social norms; disciplining those who violate the rules of a social group, and unifying other group members against them; and dividing group members from other groups (those who would be expected to adopt a different perspective; e.g. see Meyer, 2000). It is unclear whether the gurus and their audiences can be classified as members of distinctive social groups. Indeed, part of the management gurus' mission is to recruit managers to such groups, whose boundaries are defined by reference to their members' affiliation with the gurus' theories. Nonetheless, by evoking and producing laughter, the gurus and their audience members engage in public displays of consensus and 'like-mindedness' (Glenn, 1989, 2003) and thereby *constitute* themselves as 'in-groups' that share a common perspective in relation to the circumstances and events that the gurus describe. When gurus attack/disparage others (e.g. Peters' attack on GM in the example above), the gurus and those audience members who laugh also publicly differentiate themselves from individuals or groups who purportedly do not share the values or perspectives they are expressing. In these cases, then, humour and laughter serve to delineate group boundaries by acting as both a unifier and a divider (Meyer, 2000). Whether these publicly displayed group affiliations actually reflect audience members' commitment to the gurus' views and thus may extend beyond the lifetime of the gurus' lectures is, of course, open to question. Nonetheless, even those cases of laughter that are not open to interpretation as unvarnished expressions of support for the gurus' core ideas indicate a shared perspective and - like affiliative interactional practices in general (Goffman, 1983; Heritage, 1984) - contribute to a sense of cohesion and intimacy, which might make audiences more receptive to the gurus' recommendations.

The processes involved here have largely been overlooked in previous research due to the lack of systematic studies of the verbal and nonverbal practices that inform both the production and recognition of jocular talk and the coordination and interpretation of responses by hearers. Our CA study of management guru oratory shows that analysis of these practices provides important insights into both the situational dependency and the functions of humour in management and other settings. This is not to deny the importance of other contextual factors such as people's emotional states, and their familiarity or unfamiliarity with social scripts, cultural norms or institutional conventions. Nevertheless, detailed scrutiny of the verbal and nonverbal practices through which humorous talk and responses are organized provides unique insights into why people laugh, when they do and what social functions their laughter performs.

Step 6: Writing Up Findings

Having completed the analysis and identified how our findings contributed to knowledge, we wrote up the findings as an academic journal article entitled 'Displaying Group Cohesiveness: Humour and Laughter in the Public Lectures of Management Gurus' (Greatbatch and Clark, 2003). The article included:

- An introduction that set out our research questions and why they are important
- An overview of the academic literature on both management gurus and humour and laughter in organizational settings
- A description of our data and methodology
- A report on our findings, including data extracts that provide examples of the phenomena discussed
- A conclusion that highlights how our research contributes to the literature on management gurus and humour and laughter in organizational settings.

We also discussed the findings in a book on management guru oratory entitled *Management Speak: Why We Listen to What Management Gurus Tell Us* (Greatbatch and Clark, 2005).

CHAPTER SUMMARY

In this chapter we have explained the specific practices involved in CA research by:

- Discussing the process in terms of the following six steps: (1) data collection; (2) identifying and refining your research questions through 'unmotivated looking'; (3) transcribing your data using the system developed by Gail Jefferson (2004); (4) analysing the single case or collection of particular types of sequences that you have identified and transcribed; (5) considering how your findings contribute to knowledge and (6) writing up your findings using extracts from transcripts of recordings as examples of the phenomena you describe and locating your findings in relation to the relevant literature(s).
- Using one of our CA studies of the dissemination of management ideas on the international management lecture circuit as an example of this process.

5

EXAMPLES OF CONVERSATION ANALYTIC STUDIES

CA research on institutional talk provides a crucial resource that you can draw upon when conducting your research. However, as noted in previous chapters, there is also a growing body of CA studies in business and management research that not only contribute to the CA literature on institutional talk but also offer distinctive theoretical contributions to business and management knowledge. In this chapter, we will provide an overview of these studies and present examples that can help frame your research questions and illustrate how you can use CA to address areas of inquiry in the field of business and management. The areas we will focus on are as follows:

- Leadership and influencing
- Decision-making
- Emotion
- Performance appraisal
- Sales and service work.

LEADERSHIP AND INFLUENCING

In recent years a growing body of business and management scholars have rejected grand theories of leadership and adopted instead social constructionist, 'discursive' approaches that focus on the role of verbal and nonverbal language in constituting routine leadership practices (e.g. Baxter. 2015; Clifton, 2012; Cunliffe and Eriksen, 2011; Fairhurst, 2007; Fairhurst and Grant, 2010; Holmes and Marra, 2006; Mullany, 2011). As Baxter (2015: 2017-18) observes:

The social constructionist approach moves the locus of interest away from 'being a leader' to 'doing leadership,' which involves the judicious selection of linguistic resources for accomplishing particular leadership goals effectively. Stated simply, every time senior people open their mouths to speak, they are constructing and managing an impression of their profile as leaders (e.g. Clifton, 2012; Holmes and Stubbe, 2003).

Whereas traditional leadership research is largely concerned with the perceptions and self-reflections of leaders and attempting 'to capture the experience of leadership by forming and statistically analysing a host of cognitive, affective, and conative variables and their casual connections' (Fairhurst, 2007: 15, quoted in Choi and Schnurr, 2014), discursive leadership explores the specific process through which leadership is realized and communicated at the micro-level of interaction (e.g. Alvesson and Karreman, 2000a, 2000b; Chen, 2008; Choi and Schnurr, 2014; Clifton, 2012; Fairhurst, 2007; Schnurr and Chan, 2011).

Discursive leadership research includes a growing corpus of studies that use the approach and findings of CA to analyse leadership in action (e.g. Clifton, 2006; Larsson and Lundholm, 2013; Svennevig, 2008). The specific relevance of CA in leadership research is cogently summarized by Svennevig (2008: 535):

> CA may be considered a powerful tool for grasping the recurrent actions and interactional patterns of typical leadership events. The empirical force of CA is that it does not take the detour through what people (leaders) say they do (in interviews or questionnaires); rather, it investigates what they do in practice in various situations.

An example of a CA study of discursive leadership is Larsson and Lundholm's (2013) analysis of leadership in work interactions at a local branch of a large international bank operating in Sweden, which is summarized in Box 5.1.

Box 5.1 Leadership in work interactions in an international bank

Larsson, M. and Lundholm, S.E. (2013) 'Talking work in a bank: a study of organizing properties of leadership in work interactions'. *Human Relations*, 66 (8): 1101-29.

Overview

This CA study involves an analysis of an audio recording of a single work episode, which was conducted as part of a study of leadership in local branches of a large international bank operating in Sweden. The study demonstrates how business and management researchers can use CA to reveal and systematically analyse the largely tacit micro-level processes through which leadership and interpersonal influence are accomplished in and through talk-in-interaction in organizational settings.

Data

The study was part of a wider ethnographic research project undertaken by Larsson and Lundholm in 12 local branches of the bank. Having conducted an initial round of interviews at all 12 branches, Larsson and Lundholm interviewed and 'shadowed' managers in five branches via direct observation of their work and, in some cases, audio-recorded meetings and informal interactions in these branches. These everyday interactions struck them as being potentially important occasions for leadership and they therefore selected a number of examples for closer examination. The examples involved interactions in which Larsson and Lundholm believed influence took place, with future events concerning organizational tasks taking a different turn as a result of this. This study focuses on one of these episodes, which Larsson and Lundholm analysed using the approach and findings of CA. The study therefore represents an example of a single case analysis which, as we explained in Chapter 3, is an alternative option to collection-based studies that systematically compare episodes drawn from multiple recordings.

Findings

The example involves an exchange between a private client manager and a colleague in an open-plan office in a large branch of the bank. The private client manager is reviewing a list of deviances (such as overdrawn accounts, unpaid mortgages, etc.) in relation to customer accounts. She receives these automatically generated reports every week, checks each item and, if needed, takes appropriate action. In this case, she walks over to a male colleague's desk, shows him the list (which is on a sheet of paper) and remarks that a customer has exceeded their credit limit. Her colleague recognizes the customer immediately and he informs her that he is responsible for the customer's loans and credits, while another employee is responsible for the customer's investments. The private client manager emphasizes that he is responsible for this issue and asks him to suggest a possible course of action. Initially he suggests that he simply call the customer and alert him that the credit was overdrawn, seemingly troubled by the private client manager's intervention in his customer relationship. However, the private client manager questions the technical details about how the security for the customer's credit is set up. During this discussion they come to agree that the issue requires further investigation and devise a course of action that her colleague indicates he is committed to following, including the implication that he will report back to her with the outcome of his investigation into the issue. This course of action involves using the technicalities of the bank's credit system to make the bank's engagement with the customer more efficient for both the bank and the customer, while also generating more profit for the bank.

Larsson and Lundholm suggest that the private client manager succeeds in accomplishing interpersonal influence in four distinct ways during this encounter:

- First, she exercises influence by successfully resisting her colleague's attempts to close down the issue and thereby creates an opportunity for the issue to be reinterpreted.
- Second, she succeeds in reinterpreting the nature of the issue and the responsibilities of her colleague in a way that leaves no space for alternative interpretations and pressures her colleague to accept her perspective.
- Third, in issuing her directives (instructions) she carefully balances entitlements and demands, exhibiting a strong awareness of the relational context (see Samra-Fredericks, 2000). On several occasions, she mitigates her directives, thereby displaying attention to the need to secure legitimacy for influence to be effective.
- Fourth, she exercises influence by establishing an operational unit, which involves her working together with her colleague, as the relevant collective identity in relation to this issue. By doing so, she offers her colleague certain rights and obligations, which make him accountable for new tasks involving her preferred approach to dealing with the issue. She also uses the operational unit to provide legitimacy to some of her directives by addressing them to the 'us' of the unit rather than solely at her colleague.

Extract 5.1, below, which shows the conclusion of the interaction between the private client manager and her colleague, illustrates these points. In analysing this extract, Larsson and Lundholm look at how the construction of a plan of action regarding the overdrawn account continues, and how the interaction closes with a commitment to work in accordance with this plan from now on. Harriet (Ha) is the private client manager, Roy (Ro) is her male colleague.

Extract 5.1

190	Ro:	it means that we have made some money on him
191	Ha:	not much (2.7)
192	Ro:	no but if you disregard the wife (0.8)
		I mean I [( )]
193	Ha:	[we can't] disregard that
194	Ro:	>>then there's his son<<
195	Ha:	>>yes we'll look at him<<
196	Ro:	the whole package sort of
197	Ha:	>>yes have a look at him too<<

198 Ro: yes
199 Ha: we make SOME money on him (2.7) but (1.0) let's just fix this
issue with the <u>overdrawn limit</u> for starters
200 Ro: yes I'll start with that (.) now the son came up here
((looks at a new window on the screen))
201 Ha: ↑yes (.) yes there is too if we want to there (3.1)
202 >>yes you can<< <u>take</u> what you <u>like</u> ((leaves Rolf's desk))

Larsson and Lundholm (2013: 1119) analyse this extract as follows:

In turn 190, Roy claims that the bank has 'made some money' on this customer. This can be heard as an assertion of his competency, in the face of the criticism implied by Harriet's attention to the overdrawn account. In terms of categorizations, it can be heard as a claim that working towards profit for the bank (rather than just following rules) is a predicate of an account manager (much in line with the general culture of the bank, valuing professionalism and personal relationships above rule-based behaviour). The interactional function of this utterance can thus be seen as a claim for a certain amount of discretion, by expanding his moral obligations beyond following rules.

Harriet disagrees (turn 191), but her disagreement refers to the size of the profit, not the obligation to focus on profit. The disagreement is solved in turn 196 by Roy suggesting that they look at 'the whole package', in essence widening the scope of what he is to do and what the solutions might be, again echoing the claim for autonomy and discretion.

In turn 199, Harriet initiates the actual closing of the interaction. The relevance of profit is acknowledged, followed by a summary of the primary task to be solved: the overdrawn credit. This is what needs to be done 'for starters', leaving room for discretion and autonomy in looking into the matter (hearably referring to 'the whole package'). Further, despite that the request to 'fix this issue' hearably is a directive to Roy, the subject is 'us', that is, the collective identity of Roy and Harriet. Roy's obligations in working with the task are thus directed towards this collective identity and towards Harriet.

Roy responds affirmatively, displaying commitment to engage with the task. Commenting on what comes up on the screen works to display that he is in fact already doing it. In her final turn, Harriet's comment on what is on the screen can be heard as an acknowledgement of his commitment, and she ends the conversation with what might be understood as an expression of trust in what Roy does. The interaction ends, but what remains are the new obligations for Roy, as incumbent of the category of account manager, to engage with the task as constructed here. The organizing process thus has resulted in work that stretches beyond the boundaries of the interaction as such.

Conclusions

Larsson and Lundholm explain that their single-case analysis of leadership and influence in action contributes to business and management theory in four ways:

- First, it contributes to knowledge by adding to the findings of research which has shown how an important aspect of organizing is struggle for and accomplishment of spatio-temporal closures (e.g. Cooren and Fairhurst, 2004; Taylor and Robichaud, 2007). Specifically, it shows how leadership also opens up and keeps issues open, thereby creating new occasions for sensemaking (Weick, 1995), thus permitting future flexibility to enable new understandings to emerge and new organizing processes to be set in motion.
- Second, while it is commonly accepted that leadership entails influence directed towards organizationally relevant tasks (Rost, 1991; Yukl, 2002), in line with Fairhurst's (2007) argument for leadership practices as interactional and highly situated, their analysis demonstrates how the construction of a specific and situated version of a more general task is central to the organizing process. This construction is enabled through the above-mentioned opening up of issues, and is accomplished through further delicate interactional work.
- Third, their analysis adds to the existing arguments about the centrality of interdependencies for organizing processes. Rather than behaviours (Weick, 1979) or types of actions and types of actors (Tsoukas and Chia, 2002), they emphasize interactional identities as the elements that are made interdependent. Interdependencies are established through reconstructions of the obligations associated with the interactional identities (Hester and Eglin, 1997; Jayyusi, 1984; Sacks, 1992). Organizing can here be said to occur when the participants establish mutual obligations in relation to the task at hand.
- Fourth, and perhaps most importantly, their study shows the influence and organizing functions of a situated collective identity. Rather than individual identities organizing action (Pye, 2005; Weick, 1995), we see here the collective identity of an operational unit playing a central role in the organizing process. It is through the establishment of this collective identity that individual interactional identities are endowed with new obligations, rendering them interdependent. The establishment of a task-based rather than generalized collective identity (Gardner and Avolio, 1998; Taylor and van Every, 2010) can thus be seen as one of the primary organizing functions of leadership. It entails the reconstruction of a task and the suggestion that 'we' work on it together.

DECISION-MAKING

Organizational research has largely concerned rational models of decision-making which favour logic, objectivity and analysis over subjectivity and insight. Rational decision-making consists of a series of steps (see March, 1994), for example:

- Define the nature of the decision to be made in relation to a problem or opportunity (step 1)
- Identify decision criteria (step 2)
- Collect pertinent information (step 3)
- Identify alternative courses of action (step 4)
- Weigh all the evidence (step 5)
- Select an alternative (step 6)
- Take action (step 7)
- Review results of the decision and assess whether or not it has resolved the need identified at the outset of the process (step 8).

As Clifton (2009: 60) observes: 'Such rational models of decision making therefore consider it to be an asocial, cognitive action, and the interactive forum in which decisions are actually made has tended to be overlooked.' In view of this, various researchers (Boden, 1994; Clifton, 2009; Huisman, 2001; Schwartzman, 1989) have argued that there is a need for research which examines the process of real time decision-making in workplace interaction. There is a quite extensive CA literature on this topic. These studies concern mainly, although not exclusively, business meetings (Asmuß and Svennevig, 2009; Svennevig, 2012), focusing on particular management styles (Schmitt, 2006), managers' interpretative work (Nielsen, 2009), enactment of leadership (Clifton, 2006; Svennevig, 2008) and chairing (Pomerantz and Denvir, 2007), negotiation of participants' mutual influence (Clifton, 2009), facilitation of agreement (Barnes, 2007), the collaborative construction of a commitment to future action that constitutes a decision (Huisman, 2001) and use of politeness (Wasson, 2000). These studies indicate that influencing decision-making is not a question of acting rationally in a cognitive sense but it is rather one of effectively using discourse resources at one's disposal to influence and gain commitment to a course of future action. This is informed by the participants' orientation to what they perceive as allowable contributions to the talk that allows certain participants to have greater influence in the decision-making process' (Clifton, 2009: 61).

A study that exemplifies the CA approach to understanding decision-making is Huisman's (2001) examination of decision-making in meetings in four Dutch organizations, which is summarized in Box 5.2.

Box 5.2 Decision-making in management meetings

Huisman, M. (2001) 'Decision-making in meetings as talk-in-interaction'. *International Studies of Management & Organization*, 31 (3): 69–90.

Overview

Defining a decision as a 'commitment to future action', Huisman shows that in order to understand how a decision is made it is necessary to examine: the interactional processes through which it is defined, discussed and made; the cultural norms of a group and/or organization which shape the specific interactional procedures that contribute to a 'decision'; and the subjective dimensions of decision-making, whereby the identity of participants contributes to the specific patterns of interaction that emerge.

Data

Huisman's data mainly comprise video recordings of 12 management meetings, totalling just over 37 hours, held in three different Dutch organizations. These involve four successive meetings of three teams: a senior management team of an information and communications technology company; a management team of a service department in a university hospital; and a board of directors of a higher professional education institution. In addition to these three organizations, Huisman also analysed an audio recording of an important meeting of teaching staff at a Dutch high school and gathered additional data through interviews and participant observation.

Huisman's article uses extracts that have been translated from Dutch to English, with the original Dutch extracts included in an appendix.

Findings

Huisman presents four decision-making episodes to highlight several issues, which include:

- Decision-making in meetings is accomplished through collaborative and interactional processes within talk-in-interaction.
- In some cases it can remain unclear whether in fact a decision has been made. Some people contend that a decision has been made in a meeting, even though it has not been explicitly formulated and other people contest this interpretation of events.
- What counts as a decision will be largely dependent upon the norms and patterns of behaviour of the particular group or organization under study; that is, decision-making is context sensitive.

By way of example, consider Extract 5.2 below, which Huisman uses to illustrate how decisions in meetings emerge through an 'interactional process in which participants jointly construct the formulation of a state of affairs, and through further assessment and formulation build commitment to particular future states of affairs' (Huisman 2001: 75). This extract is taken from the end of a decision-making episode in a meeting of the head management team of the ICT company mentioned above. Seven managers are in attendance. Jaap, chair and general manager, Marcel, manager of the operations department, and Karel, head of the financial control department, are involved in this extract. Prior to the episode included in the extract, the management team had decided that someone from Marcel's department (Mehmet) would be invited along with someone from Karel's department to discuss financial matters with the team.

Extract 5.2

(PMX is a term that is part of the specific terminology of the company under study)

```
1   Marcel:   those are the PMX-es hey
2             that is of course after the decimal ↑point
3             that's one point fou[r ↑million
4   Jaap:                        [no but wait
5   Marcel:   [while we (talk) here about eight million.
6   Jaap:     [who runs >>in your<< is that uh
7   Jaap:     d-do we need (Klaas) for [that?
8   Karel:    [n(h)o (Margaret)
9   Marcel:   [(Margaret).
10  Jaap:     [(Margaret).
11            ok[ay (Margaret) with (Mehmet)
12  Marcel:       [you (go-)
```

Huisman (2001: 75-6) analyses this fragment as follows:

In this fragment, Jaap proposes a part of the future state of affairs that the team wants to create: he proposes to invite Klaas from Karel's department (line 7). Karel rejects this proposal. After his negative assessment ('n(h)o,' line 8) he formulates an alternative ('Margaret'). This gets confirmed by Marcel and Jaap (lines 9-11). In this small episode we not only see the interactive construction of commitment, but also the interactive construction of part of the future state of affairs that is to be created.

In this way, a decision in a meeting is a product of an interactional process in which participants jointly construct the formulation of states of affairs, and through further assessment and formulation build commitment to particular future states of affairs. Apart from that decisions cannot be attributed to one specific utterance, but rather are emergent, it is important to notice that decisions do not necessarily get explicated as such. Participants could, of course, explicate decisions in the interaction. For instance the chair of the meeting could say something like 'then we decide to buy the machine'. Such a formulation would label the preceding episode retrospectively as a decision (Heritage and Watson 1979). However, in the data we studied, these explicating formulations were very rare.

Although we can study decision-making episodes, these episodes should, of course, be placed in the context of a continuous stream of decision-making that develops in organizations in a variety of settings. A decision-making episode of a meeting is a snapshot of developing and constantly reviewing courses of action in organizations. Furthermore, not every attempt of participants to arrive at a formulation of a future state of affairs and a commitment to create it results in a decision. In other words decision-making episodes can end without resulting in a decision. The topic can be picked up later in a different setting, or can just leave the stage. Moreover, decisions can be modified or called off at a later time or in a different setting, while a general commitment to them can be extended and reinforced (Mintzberg and Waters 1990, p.4).

Conclusions

Huisman demonstrates that decision-making is not only bounded rationally, as in Herbert Simon's (1976) classic model of decision processes, but is also socially and linguistically constructed in talk-in-interaction. In her view, CA therefore offers a powerful tool to explore how managers formulate and justify decisions and shape their organization's potential future. Huisman concludes by highlighting the importance of confronting decision-making theories with empirical studies of the actual interactional processes through which decisions are accomplished in talk-in-interaction in organizations.

EMOTION

Until recently, the emotional behaviour of organizational actors was rarely considered in organizational studies. One reason for this was that organizational researchers generally regarded emotion as the opposite of rationality and this led to a negative perception of emotion (Ashforth and Humphrey, 1995; Fineman, 2000, 2003; Kangasharju and Nikko, 2009). However, it is now widely recognized that emotions play an important role in organizations and that, far from being the opposite of each other, rationality and emotion are interconnected in many different ways (Ashforth and Humphrey, 1995; Fineman, 2000; Madlock, 2008).

Research on emotion in organizations often focuses on affective states such as boredom, satisfaction or stress, or positive or negative feelings, which have been examined through interviews in which people describe their emotions. This research has been criticized for neglecting both the context of the emotional experiences and the impact of the interviewing situation on the descriptions elicited (Kitzinger and Frith, 1999). This has led researchers to study emotion directly in organizations using, for example, participant observation (Fineman, 1999, 2000) and, to a lesser extent, CA.

CA offers a distinctive and important approach to research on emotions in that rather than focusing on emotions as internal states or experiences, it examines *displays* of emotions – such as enjoyment, frustration, embarrassment, disgust, disbelief, anger, horror and amazement – in talk-in-interaction, examining how these are accomplished and coordinated, and how they can open up alternative trajectories for sequences-in-progress (Sundland, 2004). These displays of emotion may be accomplished through facial expressions, laughter, tone of voice/prosody, lexical choices and/or gestures and bodily movements. CA can also be used to examine sequences in which people describe/refer to their own emotions or the emotions of others.

One form of emotional behaviour in an organizational context that has attracted the attention of researchers using CA is joint laughter. The authors' work on collective laughter in management guru lectures, which we summarized in the previous chapter, is one example. Another example is Adelswärd and Öberg's (1998) study of business meetings involving companies negotiating with other organizations. They found that joint laughter was a boundary marker between the different phases of the negotiation activity, and it was also used to signal what topics were regarded as important or sensitive. More recently, Kangasharju and Nikko (2009) examined joint laughter in internal meetings in two large Finnish–Swedish corporations. Their study is summarized in Box 5.3.

Box 5.3   Joint laughter in workplace meetings

Kangasharju, H. and Nikko, T. (2009) 'Emotions in organizations: joint laughter in workplace meetings'. *Journal of Business Communication*, 46: 100–19.

Overview

Kangasharju and Nikko analyse examples of joint laughter in meetings between cross-border teams following the merger of two large Swedish and Finnish corporations. They demonstrate that joint laughter occurs in conjunction with specific activities during the meetings and is not necessarily associated with humour. Their results support the findings of previous research studies that argue that shared laughter is a means through which participants can reduce hierarchical asymmetry, release tension in challenging situations, increase feelings of close-ness and collegiality and/or alleviate face-threatening or embarrassing situations (Ashforth and Humphrey, 1995; Glenn, 1989; Greatbatch and Clark, 2003, 2005; Haakana, 1999).

Data

Kangasharju and Nikko's data comprised approximately 16 hours of video record-ings of five cross-border meetings of regular teams, where the participants used English as a common language. The recordings were made soon after the merger of the Finnish and Swedish units. The length of the meetings varied from one hour to almost six hours, and the number of participants varied between four and ten.

Drawing on Boden's (1994) distinction between formal and informal meetings, Kangasharju and Nikko characterize the meetings as semiformal. The formal char-acteristics of the meetings include large numbers of participants, the use of a chairperson and a fixed agenda. The informal characteristics include a casual con-versation style. The meetings were primarily concerned with sharing information or solving joint problems.

Findings

Kangasharju and Nikko (2009: 105) address the following research questions, which they formulated having reviewed and identified gaps in the literature:

1. What different functions does joint laughter have in leader–member meetings?
2. What kind of activities in the meeting is the joint laughter connected to?
3. How are the laughing sequences constructed by the meeting participants, and what kind of interactional practices do they use when accomplishing this activity?

Kangasharju and Nikko found that shared laughter during the meetings was connected to the accomplishment of tasks that can be regarded as challenging, regardless of whether the laughter was associated with humour and amusement. This feature dis-tinguishes the joint laughter occurring in these organizational meetings from laughter in mundane contexts, where joint laughter occurs in a large variety of situations.

Kangasharju and Nikko identify four main functions for joint laughter in the meetings.

*   First, managers and team leaders invited shared laughter associated with humour to create a relaxed working climate and to reduce asymmetry and tension between the team members. This was especially apparent during the openings of the meetings, particularly those at a high hierarchical level. Kangasharju and

Nikko note that this finding empirically confirms Ashforth and Humphrey's (1995) theoretical claim that leaders can use humour and laughter strategically in meetings with their subordinates to reduce tension.

- Second, joint laughter was associated with the closure of topics or phases of a meeting in a way that involves the participants, through laughter, in public displays of consensus and 'like-mindedness' (Glenn, 1989; Greatbatch and Clark, 2003). In these cases, joint laughter – which was invited by both team leaders and team members – functions to display that the participants share a mutual understanding of the issue at hand (see also Adelswärd and Öberg, 1998; Haakana, 1999).

- Third, team members sometimes invited joint laughter to reduce stress and tension linked to demanding task assignments. Kangasharju and Nikko found that team members invited joint laughter in ways that were different from managers. Whereas the managers often created a 'one-to-many' or 'entertainer–audience' communicative event (see Glenn, 1989), team members were more likely to invite their co-participants to jointly construct and contribute to the development of the humorous items.

- A fourth important function of shared laughter was accomplishing remedial work in a problematic or face-threatening situation. Kangasharju and Nikko give the example of team members inviting joint laughter in a situation where the team leader might lose face.

Extract 5.3, below, exemplifies how managers chairing meetings may seek to evoke shared laughter to create a more relaxed atmosphere during the openings of the meetings.

Extract 5.3

```
01  Ch ->   Well (.) you all know that times are changing if you
02          look at the (.) er- different let's say (.) teevee
03          programs (.) There is a new sort of trend (.) with
04          these (.) er- live soap operas
05          (.)
06  Kauko   [Mm.]
07  Ch->    [In  ] Sweden there's a big one now going on called
08          the Bar (.) About ten people operating a bar in
09          Stockholm and living together in a flat. (.) We're
10          not going to live together but this the first (.)
11          first program of the company
12          (.)
13  Kauko   Mm.
```

```
14   Ch->     er- which is recorded today. (.) It's going to be
15            sent live on internet all over the world.
16            -> ((joint laughter))
17   Antti    Direct yeah.
18   Ch->     Expected audience zero.
19            -> ((joint laughter))
20   Ch ->    Might be someone in XX Company ((= a competitor))
21            who will be forced to look at it.
22            -> ((joint laughter))
23   Kauko    Do you [do] you think we beat [the ] O J Simpson's
24   Ch - >        [So]                    [(−)]
25   Kauko    jury trial?
26   Ch - >   Could be. ((moves to the issues at hand))
```

Kangasharju and Nikko's (2009: 107–8) analysis of this extract is as follows:

(This extract) illustrates a manager's endeavors to lighten the atmosphere of the meeting and to create a feeling of collegiality and solidarity in the opening phase of a meeting. The meeting is held in Finland and there are nine participants present, representing three nationalities, Finns, Swedes and Germans. The chair is Swedish, and he is the manager of the whole group. Ashforth and Humphrey (1995), who have investigated emotional behavior in organizations, claim that it is the primary task of the managers to create and sustain shared meanings as well as to put effort on measures that help the members of the organization to proceed in the same direction. In conjunction with organizational changes such as mergers and acquisitions, this endeavor is extremely important and can be called 'creating a fellow-feeling'.

The researchers further claim that creating a fellow-feeling is rather accomplished through symbolic actions than through direct verbal utterances. For example, saying 'We are like a big family' sounds naive and manipulative. A better solution would be, for example, to have a party together. Activities such as laughter, play, and humor may also work well. This is precisely what is done in (this extract). After having moved from an initial small talk phase to the meeting proper (transcript not given here), the manager introduces a telling sequence (lines 1–21) in which he compares the video filming of the meeting to a reality television show. The comparison invites joint laughter from the members of the group three times (lines 16, 19, and 22).

Laughter sequences can be initiated with several forms of invitation, one of which is producing a 'laughable' (Jefferson et al., 1987).

In (this extract), the comparison made by the chair functions as a laughable. Laughter sequences can be further extended by producing additional laughables. This also happens in (this extract): the Finnish participants extend the humorous description through their remarks (lines 17, 23 and 25), which can be heard as reinforcement of the (Swedish) manager's effort. A special trick that can be assumed to further increase the feeling of collegiality is the manager's reference to a 'common enemy' (i.e., the competitor, lines 20-21).

Conclusions

Kangasharju and Nikko conclude that the functions of shared laughter in the meetings form a continuum. At one end of this continuum participants invite laughter through various humorous elements, with joint laughter typically functioning to engender and display a feeling of shared interest and understanding and lighten the atmosphere, especially in the opening phases of the meetings of new groups (see also Ashforth and Humphrey, 1995). At the other end of the continuum is joint laughter that seems to be an almost obligatory element that functions to mitigate challenging and face-threatening situations. Between these two poles of the continuum is joint laughter that appears to combine both these functions.

Kangasharju and Nikko found that joint laughter that is perceived as a humorous activity related to a jocular mode is often extended through additional elements by the other participants. In contrast, joint laughter associated with problematic issues, though affiliative, tends to be short and not extended through extra elements. Nonetheless, they note that all the episodes of joint laughter in their database display co-operativeness and collegiality, thereby promoting effective communication and thus improving the task performance of the persons involved and, ultimately, the achievement of the goals of the organization.

PERFORMANCE APPRAISAL

Performance appraisal interviews are regular strategic interviews between a manager and an employee that focus on employee performance and development. They are also sometimes referred to as employee performance appraisals, job appraisal interviews, employee reviews and employee appraisals. Because performance appraisal interviews are used to determine career development and training needs of the workforce, they are critical to the effective use of human capital and they have been the focus of much research, designed to examine themes such as employee satisfaction, added organizational value and best practice (Asmuß, 2008). However, relatively little of this research examines what actually happens in the performance appraisal interview itself (e.g. Asmuß,

2008, 2013; Kikoski, 1998; Kikoski and Litterer, 1983). In view of this a number of researchers have recently examined performance appraisal interviews through the analytic lens of CA. These researchers provide unique insights into the communicative practices that are used by managers and employees in the context of critical feedback, discussion of employees' problems and other aspects of performance appraisal interviews.

Thus, for example, Asmuß's (2008) influential study examined the delicate task of how critical feedback is managed in performance appraisal interviews. The way negative feedback is given is predominantly through negative assessments, which represent a socially problematic action according to research on ordinary talk-in-interaction (Pomerantz, 1984). Asmuß (2008) found that the more the supervisor shows an orientation to negative assessments as being socially problematic, the more difficult it becomes for the employee to deal with negative assessments. Building on Asmuß' (2008) work, Clifton (2012) focuses on the communicative strategies deployed by practitioners to deal with performance appraisal interviews that risk their losing face, while Scheuer (2014) examines employees' talk about problems in work. Scheuer's study is summarized in Box 5.4 below.

Box 5.4   Performance appraisal interviews

Scheuer, J. (2014) 'Managing employees' talk about problems in work in performance appraisal interviews'. *Discourse Studies*, 16 (3): 407–29.

Overview

Scheuer examines how employees' talk about problems at work is organized in talk-in-interaction in performance appraisal meetings, paying particular attention to the stance adopted by supervisors and how this can limit the extent to which problems are discussed while allowing supervisors to use their authority to define problems and solutions.

Data

Scheuer's database consists of audio recordings of 35 performance appraisal interviews in Danish companies; the recordings were made by the participants themselves. The performance appraisal interviews largely comprise a series of question–answer–response sequences. Supervisors routinely ask questions, using interview guides or preparation forms (completed by employees prior to the performance appraisal interviews), which they keep visible and work through step by step. In answering the supervisors' questions, employees relate their experiences and describe the details and conditions of their work activities. Scheuer analyses 47 instances in which this involves employees identifying problems at work.

Findings

Scheuer's key findings concern the ways in which supervisors respond to employees' descriptions of problems they are experiencing at work.

Giving advice versus proffering a remedy

Scheuer reports that supervisors' responses to employees' answers which highlight problems at work fall into two categories: giving advice and proffering a remedy. He observes that while proffering a remedy may be redefined as a form of advice, remedies are more powerful; they do away with troublesome issues. Consequently, he contends that remedies constitute the authoritative response, displaying the supervisor's superior position. This is especially apparent in cases in which supervisors present remedies as self-evident and thereby redefine problems as the employee's fault. This observation fits in well with the fact that employees accept advice very readily. In such cases, it seems that by proffering remedies supervisors potentially claim authority to dismiss criticisms altogether.

Listening to and supporting employees' voices

Scheuer notes that supervisors listen carefully to and support employees' voices by creating an environment in which they can freely talk about their experiences and concerns at work. Employees are invited to talk at length on topics identified in topic guides and preparation forms, while supervisors limit themselves to giving minimal responses (such as 'mm' and 'yeah') and taking notes. Scheuer suggests that this involves employees adopting the stance of a witness presenting their subjective view on work, while the supervisor adopts the stance of a neutral observer of the employee's talk.

Subsequently, supervisors respond to employees' answers by offering advice or remedies, neither of which promote further talk about the problems raised in the employees' answers. Rather, they settle the matter. Thus, although employees are able to raise important issues regarding work, such issues do not become topics for ensuing talk: 'Talk about problems in work is not treated as talk raising issues, but rather as requests for solutions. Regarding exploring employees' concerns, then, this pattern seems counterproductive. It occasions participants' neglect of issues in employees' talk.' (p.417).

Restoring entitlements

In offering advice in the form of directives, supervisors take on the role of experts. By offering and supporting positive prediction they occupy superior vantage points, that is, vantage points allowing them to foretell future events. The supervisor's responses induce a discrete differentiation of social roles.

Employees' talk about problems at work apparently challenges the status quo with regard to organizational entitlements. This is evident from the ensuing actions. Supervisors respond by exercising epistemic and deontic authority, that is, the right to knowledge and the right to determine others' actions (Drew and Heritage, 1992b; Stevanovic and Peräkylä, 2012). Employees subsequently show acceptance of the stance taken by supervisors and thereby cooperate in accomplishing supervisors' attempts to re-establish their own organizational entitlements in relation to knowledge and the actions of employees (Asmuß and Oshima, 2012).

In his analysis of Extract 5.4 below, Scheuer (2014) highlights several of the phenomena identified above, including supervisors' adoption of a stance of 'neutral observer' producing positive predictions. The extract opens with the employee pointing to an agenda item on a preparation form for the performance appraisal interview which refers to her main interests at work.

Extract 5.4

1		(2.2)
2	E	right and then this about what are
3		my main interests
4		you know I think it is pretty
5		cool to get to do some analyses myself
6		and get to=
7	S	=↓mm↑
8		(0.5)
9		erm and I do hope we get to do that
10	S	mm
11		(0.6)
12		you know I think I'm drowning a bit
13		in all that literature
14	S	mm=
15	E	= erm
16		(0.6)
17	E	so I would like to some more to be
18	S	mm
19	E	allowed to sit by myself and do some
20		(1.5)
21	E	and be able to see some results=
22	S	=yeah ((inhaling))
23	E	of erm
24	S	°well you will too°.
25	E	yes

```
26        (1.4)
27  E     erm
28        (3.3)
29  E     yes
30        (1.0)
```

Scheuer's (2014: 410–13) analysis of this extract is as follows:

The employee allocates space for giving an account and subsequently accounts for her preference for obtaining analytic results, and her frustration with reading scholarly literature and doing too little analysis (see lines 12–21). The account is given in a number of consecutive turns forming a multi unit turn, or discourse unit.

The supervisor contributes by producing continuers (lines 7, 10, 14, 18). Otherwise, his response is sparse. He gives no signals of affiliation or other clues to how the employee's talk is received. It may be argued that there are reasons to expect an affiliating response. The employee talks about problems coping with the amount of literature involved in work (lines 12–13). At such a point in a troubles-telling, (an) affiliating response (from co-interactions routinely) occurs (Jefferson, 1988: 428f). (Consequently), (s)ince the employee is reporting on troublesome personal experiences, (an) affiliating response would generally speaking be a preferred next (Jefferson, 1984: 211; Sacks, 1987/1973).

In comparison with informal everyday conversation, the supervisor's participation may therefore be perceived as markedly minimal. Such non-affiliative behavior is a general characteristic of interaction in work encounters (Drew and Heritage, 1992: 24). As pointed out by several authors, non-participation may be considered a display of objectivity and professionalism (Button, 1992; cf. Atkinson, 1992: 209f; Drew and Heritage, 1992: 24; Nielsen, 2009: 40). By making the employee's speech strictly the employee's business, the supervisor attains an objective position.

The answer ends in a recapitulation; lines 17–21 sum up points made in preceding turns. This is an answer-exit device; the employee signals the completion of her answer and explicates the preference for a response (Pomerantz, 1984). The supervisor acknowledges the answer in line 22 and briefly takes the floor.

The response is given in line 24. It is a positive prediction foretelling improvement. (...) Positive prediction may be regarded as talk at work somewhat in parallel to what Jefferson refers to as optimistic projection in everyday troubles-telling (Jefferson, 1988). Optimistic projection refers to expressing hopes of improvement. Positive prediction refers to pointing to upcoming bettering conditions of work. Optimistic projection occurs regularly during troubles-telling(s) and in (this) context it (generally implicates closure of discussion of troubles) (Jefferson, 1988: 431ff). It seems that this (holds) for positive prediction in the present context. The employee does not self-select thereafter. By assuring the employee that her wishes will be fulfilled it seems that the supervisor leaves her nothing more to say. In terms of bringing forth employees' stances on problems, then, this type of response seems to be of dubious value.

Conclusions

The study reveals how supervisor authority is established and maintained on a turn-by-turn basis in performance appraisal interviews and how this operates to limit the extent to which participants discuss issues raised in employee answers. Scheuer asserts that this is inconsistent with the prescriptions of the literature on management communication, which suggest that employee voices should be carefully listened to and supported.

SALES AND SERVICE WORK

Every day, across the world, large numbers of sales and service employees interact with customers and clients in encounters that occur in person, over the telephone or via the Internet. Business and management researchers have sought to expand understanding of satisfying and successful sales and service encounters by examining, for example, 'whether customer expectations differ from what contact employees believe customers desire from the service encounter' (Kania and Gruber, 2013). Studies have been conducted in a range of sectors, including consulting, engineering, government, health care, information technology, manufacturing, professional services and not-for-profit.

CA enables researchers to explore the interactional practices through which employees and customers/clients coordinate their conduct and interpret each other's actions in real time during sales and service encounters. CA researchers have examined a range of different types of sales and service encounter, including calls to emergency services (Whalen et al., 1988) and telemedicine services (Greatbatch et al., 2005); telephone sales (Clark et al., 1994; Mazeland, 2004); and business-to-business selling (Clark et al., 2003). These studies demonstrate the value of using CA in these contexts, especially in terms of showing how employees: deal with local contingencies by working around attempts to standardize their work routines; establish and deal with customer and client expectations as service encounters unfold in real time; and manage (effectively or otherwise) practical and interactional problems. The studies also show the importance of considering the role that customers play in shaping work tasks, an issue that has to date attracted relatively little systematic analytical attention (Llewelyn and Hindmarsh, 2013).

Oshima's (2014) study of Japanese service encounters in hairdressing salons illustrates how CA can been used to analyse service encounters in the business and management field. It also provides an example of how CA can be used to analyse non-verbal communication. Oshima's study is summarized in Box 5.5.

Box 5.5   The role of nonverbal communication in service encounters in Japan

Oshima, S. (2014) 'Achieving consensus through professionalized head nods: the role of nodding in service encounters in Japan'. *Journal of Business Communication*, 51 (1): 31–57.

Overview

The study examines hair salon interactions in Japan focusing on the service-assessment sequence, where the hairstylist and customer inspect the completed work and deter-mine whether it is adequate. The study reveals how in Japan synchronized heading nodding plays a key role in achieving consensus in these service encounters, and discusses how such practices may contribute to bringing the encounters to satis-factory closure and may help retain clients. The study also compares the features of service-assessment sequences in hair salons in Japan with those in recordings of interactions between hair stylists and customers in hair salons in the United States.

Data

The video recordings of interaction in hair salons in Japan feature five stylists (two male and three female stylists) and six customers (five female and one male), and are drawn from 30 video-recorded sessions at nine different beauty salons col-lected in Japan in 2007. Each session was videotaped in its entirety with sessions ranging in length from less than 30 minutes to up to three hours (e.g. for colouring and/or perms).

The sessions began with an exchange of greetings between the stylist and the customer, followed by a consulting session, hair wash, cutting/colouring/perming, drying and styling. All the sessions included service-assessment sequences, dur-ing which hairstylists and customers established whether or not aspects of the new haircut and ultimately the finished haircut were adequate. So, for example, service-assessment sequences were sometimes found before a stylist moved from one session (e.g. cutting) to another (e.g. drying/styling) and all the sessions ended following a service assessment sequence focused on the adequacy of the haircut as a whole.

One common element found in hair salons in Japan and the United States visited by Oshima was the use of two mirrors: a large, fixed mirror towards the front of the participants and a hand-held mirror, usually set aside for evaluation or viewing of hard-to-see areas. In Japan the customers did not hold the hand-held mirror on their own, whereas in the United States customers themselves held the hand-held mirror to look at the back of their haircuts. In Japan the stylists position the hand-held mirror behind their customers who face forward, towards the large, fixed mirror. Stylists typically first showed one side of the back of the haircut and then moved the hand-held mirror to reflect the other side.

Findings

Oshima found that the participants ended the service-assessment sequence with a set of synchronized head movements, which conveyed consensus that the hair cut was satisfactory. When they failed to achieve synchronization of their head nods, customers created another opportunity to synchronize their nods with those of the stylists. In some cases, participants were able to complete the service-assessment sequence despite having limited verbal resource available.

Oshima suggests that head nodding practices were a particularly useful resource given that stylists and clients had limited options available to communicate through gaze, gestures or other bodily movements. Clients sat in their chairs typically with their hands placed on their laps and therefore could not practise noticeable gaze-shifts either, as they sat looking straight ahead into the fixed mirror in order to view their haircut in the reflection from the hand-held mirror that the stylists (whose reflection they could also see) held up behind them. Similarly, stylists' opportunities to gesture with their hands was limited by the fact that they were holding a portable mirror behind a customer's head, while their ability to make clear gaze shifts was inhibited because they were gazing at the customer's reflection in the large, fixed mirror. In these circumstances, head nods became an especially useful route through which to communicate nonverbally and coordinate parallel bodily movements.

The following extract is used by Oshima to demonstrate how head nodding can sometimes be the primary resource for achieving a consensus during the service-assessment sequence in Japanese salons. The extract involves a stylist and a customer who do not speak each other's language. The customer, Ethan, is an American, native English speaker, and the stylist, Ken, is a native Japanese speaker. Arrows indicate upward (↗) or downward (↘) head movements, with the sizes of the arrows indicating degrees of head movement.

Extract 5.5

```
            (01:35-01:51)
 1   Ken:   ((takes a hand-held mirror and places it behind Ethan))
 2          (0.7)
 3   Ken:   ↘
            ↗↘↘↘↘↘↘
 4   Ethan: [°nn°
 5   Ken:   [           ↗↘↘ ↘ ((moves the hand-held mirror from left to right))
 6   Ethan: °(right)°
 7   Ethan: ((aligns with Ken's movement by adjusting the position of his head))
 8          (1.3) ((Ethan and Ken continue looking at the large mirror))
 9          (4.9) ((Ethan touches the side of his haircut while Ken keeps holding
            the mirror))
            ↘
10   Ethan: °yes.°
              |__|
               |
            ((Ethan puts down his hand))
              ↗        ↘
11   Ken:   [°daijyoubu.°
            (it is) okay.
12   Ethan: [       ↘
                    |
            ((Ken starts folding the mirror))
13          ((Ethan and Ken bow concurrently))
```

Oshima's (2014: 49-50) analysis of this extract is as follows:

Ken initiates an evaluation by unfolding a hand-held mirror (line 1), and then slightly nods (line 3). His embodied actions are followed by Ethan's repetitive nods (line 4). Ken soon overlaps with Ethan by also producing repetitive nods and then slides the mirror from the left to the right (line 5). Through the use of head nods, they move the physical inspection forward to the next step, which is the evaluation of the other side of the haircut. There, Ethan spends approximately 6 seconds looking at and touching his hair (lines 8 and 9), and then nods deeply while speaking softly, 'yes' (line 10). Ethan's verbal and embodied actions are treated as an opportunity for Ken to move the sequence toward its closure, who says 'daijyoubu,' meaning '(is it) okay,' (line 11). At this moment, Ken also lifts his chin upward, indicating a stretched head nod to come. As soon as Ethan sees Ken's head movement (their head movements are visible to each other, as they are both reflected in and looking at the large mirror in front of them), Ethan nods once again (line 12). This is followed by Ken's action of folding the hand-held mirror. As a result, the sequence was organized by their close monitoring of each other's head movements, leading to a successful completion.

Conclusions

Oshima concludes by comparing the conduct of stylists and customers in the Japanese salons with that of their counterparts in salons in the United States. She found that participants in the Japanese salons used fewer verbal practices for communicating their degree of consent that haircuts were adequate – both in terms of variety and frequency. This appears to confirm a widely documented characteristic of Japanese communication style – a preference for ambiguity and indirectness – which has been highlighted in studies of Japanese business communication and has been identified as a barrier to intercultural communication when non-Japanese engage in business with Japanese (e.g. Haneda and Shima, 1982; Nishiyama, 1999; Peltokorpi, 2007). Oshima notes that these studies suggest that in order to communicate effectively with Japanese people it is necessary for non-Japanese to be able to read their inner-states (feelings and intentions) from different communicative strategies they use, for example, 'subtle nonverbal signals such as avoiding eye contact, prolonged silence, and scratching the head' (Nishiyama, 1999: 96). However, Oshima argues that her analysis indicates that these studies overemphasize the ambiguous and indirect characteristics of Japanese communication and 'may result in adding another, perhaps unnecessary, hurdle for non-Japanese to conduct business with Japanese' (Oshima, 2014: 52). She concludes:

Multimodal conversation analysis of the sequence allowed us to capture that the consensus was not made because of the participants' equipped skills of reading each other's inner-states such as their 'hidden' feelings and 'real' intentions. Rather, the participants systematically worked on creating the status of being in consensus through a constant, moment-by-moment monitoring of each other's visible movement (Oshima, 2014: 51).

DISCUSSION

Together with the CA studies of institutional interaction, CA research conducted by business and management researchers provides a rich repository of methodological and empirical insights on which you can draw in undertaking your research. These studies encompass both interactions that take place within organizations (internal communication) and those involving contact between organizational representatives and 'users' of the organization, such as customers, clients, patients, etc. (external communication).

The studies considered in this chapter use the approach and findings of CA to shine a light on what are sometimes viewed as invisible elements of organisational life. They reveal the micro, real-time interactions through which organizational tasks and activities are accomplished in a wide range of situations and, in doing so, specifically address issues that are current in business and management research. Consequently, they provide a distinct perspective and novel insights into core themes and topics within this field, while also contributing to the CA literature on institutional talk.

CHAPTER SUMMARY

In this chapter we have provided examples of CA studies which demonstrate:

- How you can use CA to address areas of inquiry in the field of business and management research
- The relevance of CA in relation to research on leadership and influencing, decision-making, emotion, performance appraisal, formality and informality in organizations, service encounters and virtual communication, amongst others
- The potential of CA to reveal the largely tacit micro-level processes through which the decisions and processes that maintain organizational life are accomplished in and through talk-in-interaction in organizational settings.

 **6**

STRENGTHS AND LIMITATIONS OF CONVERSATION ANALYSIS

INTRODUCTION

Our aim in this chapter is to ensure that you have the means to articulate a justification for using CA in your research. We begin by providing an account of the apparent limitations and challenges of using CA, paying particular attention to key criticisms that are commonly levelled at CA and how CA researchers respond to them. We then consider the strengths of CA, including the specific advantages of using this approach in the field of business and management research.

LIMITATIONS

We outline four issues that are commonly identified as limitations of CA, with some suggestions as to how you might respond to them when justifying the use of CA in your own work. These concern: CA's apparent reluctance to examine how ideology and power relations enter into talk; the fact that CA does not establish the generalizability of findings through representative samples and statistical significance; CA's restricted focus on audio and video recordings of naturally occurring talk-in-interaction; and the time required for transcription and analysis in CA studies. We briefly elaborate each of these issues below.

Ideology and Power

Some critics of CA argue that CA's attempt to ground analytic claims solely by reference to close description of the participants' conduct is too restrictive because it severely limits the ability of CA research to address issues which motivate more traditional social sciences' analysis of social interaction, such as the influences of power, class, gender and ethnicity. These critics argue that CA is too narrow and that studies of social interaction should examine how ideology and power relations enter into talk. CA researchers counter this argument by reminding the critics that CA is specifically concerned with exploring the practices that participants in talk-in-interaction use and rely upon to accomplish and coordinate social actions. That is why, from the perspective of CA, intuitively pressing issues such as power, class, gender and ethnicity issues should only feature in analysis if they can be shown to be oriented to by the participants themselves. Schegloff (1998: 416) summarizes this issue when he writes:

> Obviously some may wish to proceed differently, but it is worth recognizing that the enterprise is different and the payoffs are likely to be different in kind and in groundings as well. For CA, it is the members' world, the world of the particular members in a particular occasion, a world that is embodied and displayed in their conduct with one another, which is the grounds and the object of the entire enterprise, its *sine qua non*.

In conducting a CA study you must set aside external issues and identities, which may be relevant in an academic and/or ideological framework, and examine data and participants' orientations to one another in their own terms. This involves focusing intensely on what the participants do, the social actions they accomplish and the understandings and orientations they display to each other as their interactions unfold in real time.

The Issue of Generalizability

Social scientists who operate within the positivist paradigm emphasize the importance of establishing the generalizability of findings through representative samples, quantification and statistical significance. Often they express surprise that CA studies do not do this and suggest that this is a methodological weakness which calls into question the validity of the findings generated by CA research. From a CA perspective, however, this reflects a misunderstanding of the nature of CA studies. As we saw in Chapter 3, the ultimate goal of CA is to explicate the normative practices that participants use when organizing social interactions. Using deviant case analysis CA researchers are able to determine whether patterns of interaction comprise empirical regularities that happen to occur, or whether they arise as a result of participants using and orienting to a normative interactional rule, which is considered to be the standard way of doing something. Hoey and Kendrik (2017: 15) provide a simple and arresting example to drive home this point:

Say you build a collection of hundreds of question-answer pairs. While this would provide evidence that statistically these actions co-occur, it would not show that participants normatively expect answers to follow questions. To demonstrate normativity, you must present something like the following: (i) a question-recipient does not provide an answer, and (ii) this gets treated as problematic (the questioner pursues a response, the question-recipient accounts for the non-response, etc.). This would show that the co-occurrence of questions and answers is not merely a statistical correlation but a socially normative organization.

So, whereas in the positivist paradigm the value of research is judged by the degree to which results can be generalized to the wider population through probability sampling and statistical analysis, in CA it is judged by the extent to which findings describe normative practices, which are observably oriented to by participants in the details of their interactions.

Of course, as we have seen in Chapter 3, some CA studies do not use deviant case analysis to establish the normativity of social practices because they involve either single-case analysis or exploratory analysis of multiple cases. With regard to these studies, two points should be borne in mind. The first is that a guiding principle of CA, which has been repeatedly confirmed over the last 50 years, is that there is 'order at all points' in talk-in-interaction; this means that even if you confine your focus to a single sequence of interaction you will find phenomena that are systematically organized by the participants themselves. The second point is that CA's use of audio-visual data establishes important constraints on the quality and rigour of research by enabling social scientists to provide an independent evaluation of the strength of each other's findings by reference to the original data.

Restricted Focus on Talk-in-Interaction

An apparent limitation of CA from the perspective of business and management research is that it does not provide a framework for analysing those aspects of organizational activities that are not primarily accomplished through talk-in-interaction. For example, although key aspects of management activities such as selling and strategizing are accomplished through talk-in-interaction, these activities are likely to also involve elements that involve little in the way of talk-in-interaction and are therefore not amenable to study through the use of CA, including: email exchanges, preparation and use of documents while working alone, searching the web, and so on. Consequently, CA studies often produce a partial picture of how organizational activities and tasks are accomplished and coordinated. For most researchers, however, this is not a major concern because, as noted in Chapter 1, talk is a pervasive feature of organizational life and is emerging as a key topic of inquiry in its own right in the field of business and organizational communication. Of course, if a researcher wished to produce a 'holistic' account of a given organizational activity, which covers all the elements of which it is composed, they have the option of embedding the use of CA in a broader study that also includes the use of other methods (such as interviews, documentary analysis, observation or questionnaires) that allow them to examine aspects of an organizational activity that are not accomplished through talk-in-interaction. In so doing, however, they would need to ensure that information generated through those methods was not used to warrant claims about talk-in-interaction, which were not grounded in the understandings and orientations that interactants actually display to each other as their interactions unfold in real time.

Time Needed for Transcription and Analysis

One of the key challenges in undertaking a CA project is ensuring that it remains at an appropriate scale. Transcribing and analysing audio and video recordings thoroughly in CA studies can be very time consuming. In order to keep your study manageable you will therefore need to give careful consideration to selecting which parts of available recordings should be transcribed and analysed. This, of course, will depend on your particular research interests. If you were interested in, for example, the overall structure of a specific kind of workplace interaction (say calls to a customer services centre), it would make sense to transcribe and analyse a limited number of interactions in their entirety. On the other hand, if you are interested in a particular kind of interactional practice or phenomenon that happens every so often in a corpus of audio or video recordings, you would be well advised to transcribe only those relevant episodes. Yet again, if you are interested in understanding an unusual or unexpected occurrence (such as an encounter that degenerates into an argument or the telling of a compelling story or a reaction to an invitation that was unexpected), you could consider undertaking a single-case analysis. More generally, always remember that you should analyse your audio and video recordings while transcribing them.

Having considered some of the weaknesses that are ascribed to CA we now turn to its strengths.

STRENGTHS

The strengths of CA include: precision of observation, a stable and flexible methodology, a cumulative evidence base and an approach which aligns with key themes in the field of business and management research. We now discuss each of these points in a little more detail.

Precision of Observation

One of CA's key strengths is the precision of observation and the detail of the analysis that it facilitates. This provides access to the intricacy of human conduct, which is unavailable for systematic study by social scientific research methods that involve the analysis of field notes, interviews, responses to questionnaires or experimentally produced data. CA allows analysis to occur specifically at the fine-grained level that can be shown to be relevant to participants themselves and thereby makes explicit the normally tacit practices through which participants accomplish courses of action in real time.

Well-established and Flexible Methodology

CA's methodology has remained remarkably consistent since it was established in the foundational studies of Sacks, Schegloff and Jefferson in the 1960s and its underlying theoretical principles have been repeatedly confirmed in a burgeoning corpus of studies of naturally occurring social interaction. The methodology has proven to be sufficiently robust to make it applicable across different forms of interaction, languages, cultures and countries, as well as to the study of the role of gaze, gesture and body positioning. It has also been used in a wide range of disciplines to address disciplinary-specific topics and their associated literatures.

Another important aspect of the flexibility of CA is that the audio and video recordings that are analysed need not have been specifically collected for a particular research project. Recordings collected by organizations for quality control purposes, recordings of broadcast programmes and recordings downloaded from the web can also be used. The only proviso is that the recordings should be of naturally occurring social interaction, rather than encounters that are staged, scripted or produced under experimental conditions. Moreover, recordings can be analysed on any number of occasions, with researchers focusing on different aspects of the interactions. They can also be shown when results are presented to other academics and students. The flexibility of CA in these respects means that it provides a wide range of opportunities for research across the social sciences and that anyone who is interested in conducting a CA study can, if they wish, get hold of suitable data at little or no cost - although it is important to ensure that ethical issues and appropriate permissions are properly attended to at all times.

Cumulative Evidence Base

The robustness and quality of CA's methodology has enabled CA researchers to build a large cumulative evidence base in relation to both mundane and institutional interaction, which is methodologically coherent and provides interlocking and mutually supportive findings. This corpus of CA studies can be mined by academics and students to obtain ideas, insights and concepts; to identify gaps in the literature and ensure that they do not replicate existing studies; and to explore the contribution of their research to the existing CA literature, especially those studies undertaken by business and management researchers. They can also refer to this evidence base when conducting their analysis, for example in order to identify similarities and differences between the ways in which social actions are accomplished in different settings.

CA Aligns with Emerging Themes in Business and Management Research

CA offers a powerful and systematic approach that can be used by business and management researchers to analyse how organizational activities – such as strategizing, selling, interviewing, chairing meetings, negotiating and presenting – are accomplished and coordinated in talk-in-interaction. CA is consistent with the so-called 'discursive turn' in business and management research, which emphasizes the centrality of language in understanding the organizational world. It also chimes with the notion of the 'emergent organization', which has recently evolved into an important theme in the field of business and organizational communication and involves business and management researchers focusing on organizations as interactional accomplishments. As discussed in Chapter 3, CA scholars have been systematically exploring the ways in which organization emerges through talk-in-interaction since the 1980s and there is now a large repository of CA studies on institutional talk that shed light on this issue. These studies show how a range of organizational roles – such as interviewers–job applicants, mediators–disputants, and emergency call takers–callers – are accomplished in real time talk-in-interaction.

While CA studies of institutional talk clearly signal the potential relevance of CA for business and management research, they are not specifically concerned with the issues that preoccupy business and management researchers. However, as we saw in Chapter 5, those researchers who have used CA in studies that are explicitly focused on business and management issues demonstrate how CA can make significant theoretical contributions to a range of debates and literatures within this field.

CONCLUSION

CA opens up exciting opportunities for business and management researchers by offering a framework through which they can systematically study how organizational activities are accomplished in real time through talk-in-interaction. All too often the methods used by business and management researchers locate them at one remove from the phenomenon they are investigating or encourage them to develop a priori assumptions and so impute motives for the activities observed. In contrast, CA disciplines researchers to focus on what was said, how it was said and how interactants addressed and made sense of the unfolding talk. In so doing it reveals the invisible and taken-for-granted practices that are the essential building blocks of organizational life.

In this book we have shown you how you can use CA to analyse audio and video recordings of naturally occurring talk-in-interaction. We have described the theoretical origins and philosophical underpinnings of CA, set out the methodology, described the main steps in conducting a CA study and provided examples of CA studies in the published literature in business and management research. We have also considered the key challenges and strengths of CA and the particular benefits of using this approach in the field of business and management research. We hope you will now feel able to give serious consideration to using this approach in your own research project and come to value the critical and unique insights it provides.

REFERENCES

Adelswärd, V. and Öberg, B.-M. (1998) 'The function of laughter and joking in negotiation activities'. *International Journal of Humor Research*, 11 (4): 411-29.

Alvesson, M. and Karreman, D. (2000a) 'Varieties of discourse: on the study of organizations through discourse analysis'. *Human Relations*, 53 (9): 1125-49.

Alvesson, M. and Karreman, D. (2000b) 'Taking the linguistic turn in organizational research: challenges, responses, consequences'. *The Journal of Applied Behavioral Science*, 36 (2): 136-58.

Ashforth, B. and Humphrey, R.H. (1995) 'Emotion in the workplace: a reappraisal'. *Human Relations*, 48 (2): 97-125.

Asmuß, B. (2008) 'Performance appraisal interviews: preference organization in assessment sequences'. *Journal of Business Communication*, 45 (4): 408-29.

Asmuß, B (2013) 'The emergence of symmetries and asymmetries in performance appraisal interviews: an interactional perspective'. *Economic and Industrial Democracy*, 34 (2): 1-18.

Asmuß, B. and Oshima, S. (2012) 'Negotiation of entitlement in proposal sequences'. *Discourse Studies*, 14 (1): 67-86.

Asmuß, B. and Svennevig, J. (2009) 'Meeting talk: an introduction'. *Journal of Business Communication*, 46 (1): 3-22.

Atkinson, J.M. (1984a) *Our Masters' Voices: The Language and Body Language of Politics*. London: Methuen.

Atkinson, J.M. (1984b) 'Public speaking and audience response: some techniques for inviting applause', in J.M. Atkinson and J. Heritage (eds), *Structures of Social Action*. Cambridge: Cambridge University Press. pp. 370-409.

Atkinson, J.M. (1992) 'Displaying neutrality: formal aspects of informal court proceedings', in P. Drew and J. Heritage (eds), *Talk at Work: Interaction in Institutional Settings*. Cambridge: Cambridge University Press. pp. 199-211.

Atkinson, J.M. and P, Drew, P. (1979) *Order in Court: The Organisation of Verbal Interaction in Judicial Settings*. London: Macmillan.

Atkinson, J.M. and Heritage, J. (1984) *Structures of Social Action: Studies in Conversation Analysis*. Cambridge: Cambridge University Press.

Austin, J.L. (1962) *How to Do Things with Words*. Oxford: Oxford University Press.

Barnes, R. (2007) 'Formulations and the facilitation of common agreement in meetings talk'. *Text & Talk: An Interdisciplinary Journal of Language, Discourse & Communication Studies*, 27 (3): 273-96.

Baxter, J. (2015) 'Who wants to be the leader? The linguistic construction of emerging leadership in differently gendered teams'. *Journal of Business Communication*, 52 (4): 427-51.

Beach, W.A. (1993) 'Transitional regularities for 'casual' "Okay" usages'. *Journal of Pragmatics*, 19 (4): 325-52.

Boden, D. (1994) *The Business of Talk: Organizations in Action*. Cambridge: Cambridge Polity Press.

Button, G. (1992) 'Answers as interactional products: two sequential practices used in job interviews', in P. Drew and J. Heritage (eds), *Talk at Work: Interaction in Institutional Settings*. Cambridge: Cambridge University Press. pp. 212-34.

Chen L. (2008) 'Leaders or leadership? Alternative approaches to leadership studies'. *Management Communication Quarterly*, 21 (4): 547-55.

Choi, S. and Schnurr, S. (2014) 'Exploring distributed leadership: solving disagreements and negotiating consensus in a "leaderless" team'. *Discourse Studies*, 16 (1): 3-24.

Clark, C., Drew, P. and Pinch, T. (1994) 'Managing customer "objections" during real-life sales negotiations'. *Discourse and Society*, 5 (4): 437-62.

Clark, C., Drew, P. and Pinch, T. (2003) 'Managing prospect affiliation and rapport in real-life sales encounters'. *Discourse Studies*, 5: 5-31.

Clayman, S.E. (1992) 'Caveat orator: audience disaffiliation in the 1988 presidential debates'. *Quarterly Journal of Speech*, 78: 33-60.

Clayman, S.E. (1993) 'Booing: the anatomy of a disaffiliative response'. *American Sociological Review*, 58: 110-30.

Clayman, S.E. and Heritage, J.C. (2002) *The News Interview: Journalists and Public Figures on the Air*. Cambridge: Cambridge University Press.

Clifton, J. (2006) 'A conversation analytical approach to business communication'. *Journal of Business Communication*, 43 (3): 202-19.

Clifton, J. (2009) 'Beyond taxonomies of influence: "doing" influence and making decisions in management team meetings'. *Journal of Business Communication*, 46 (1): 57-79.

Clifton, J. (2012) 'Conversation analysis in dialogue with stocks of interactional knowledge: facework and appraisal interviews'. *Journal of Business Communication*, 49 (4): 283-311.

Clifton, J. (2014) 'Small stories, positioning, and the discursive construction of leader identity in business meetings'. *Leadership*, 10 (1): 99-11.

Cooren, F. and Fairhurst, G.T. (2004) 'Speech timing and spacing: the phenomenon of organizational closure'. *Organization*, 11 (6): 793–824.

Couper-Kuhlen, E. (2012) 'Some truths and untruths about prosody in English question and answer sequences', in J.P. de Ruiter (ed.), *Questions: Formal, Functional and Interactional Perspectives*. Cambridge: Cambridge University Press. pp.123–145.

Cunliffe, A.L. and Eriksen, M. (2011) 'Relational leadership'. *Human Relations*, 64 (11): 1425–49.

Drew, P. and Heritage, J. (eds) (1992a) *Talk at Work: Interaction in Institutional Settings*. Cambridge: Cambridge University Press.

Drew, P. and Heritage, J.C. (1992b) 'Analysing talk at work: an introduction', in P. Drew and J.C. Heritage (eds), *Talk at Work: Interaction in Institutional Settings*. Cambridge: Cambridge University Press. pp.3–65.

Fairhurst G.T. (2007) *Discursive Leadership: In Conversation with Leadership Psychology*. Los Angeles, CA: Sage.

Fairhurst, G.T. and Grant, D. (2010) 'The social construction of leadership: a sailing guide'. *Management Communication Quarterly*, 34 (2): 171–210.

Fineman, S. (1999) 'Emotion and organizing', in S.R. Clegg, S. Clegg and C. Hardy (ed:s), *Studying Organization: Theory and Method*. London: Sage. pp.289–310.

Fineman, S. (2000) *Emotion in Organizations*. London: Sage.

Fineman, S. (2003) *Understanding Emotions at Work*. London: Sage.

Fineman, S. and Sturdy, A. (1999) 'The emotions of control: a qualitative exploration of environmental regulation'. *Human Relations*, 52 (5), 631–58.

Furst, S., Blackburn, R., and Rosen, B. (1999) 'Virtual team effectiveness: a proposed research agenda'. *Information Systems Journal*, 9, 249–69.

Gardner, W.L. and Avolio, B.J. (1998) 'The charismatic relationship: a dramaturgical perspective'. *Academy of Management Review*, 23 (1): 32–58.

Garfinkel, H. (1963) 'A conception of, and experiments with, "trust" as a condition of stable concerted actions', in O.J. Harvey (ed.), *Motivation and Social Interaction: Cognitive Approaches*. New York: Ronald Press. pp.187–238.

Garfinkel, H. (1967) *Studies in Ethnomethodology*. Cambridge: Polity Press.

Glenn, P.J. (1989) 'Initiating shared laughter in multi-party conversations'. *Western Journal of Speech Communication*, 53: 127–49.

Glenn, P.J. (2003) *Laughter in Interaction*. Cambridge: Cambridge University Press.

Goffman, E. (1955) 'On face-work: an analysis of ritual elements in social interaction'. *Psychiatry*, 18 (3): 213–31.

Goffman, E. (1967) *Interaction Ritual: Essays on Face-To-Face Behavior*. New York: Anchor Books.

Goffman, E. (1981) *Forms of Talk*. Philadelphia: University of Pennsylvania Press.

Goffman, E. (1983) 'The interaction order'. *American Sociological Review*, 48 (1): 1–17.

Goodwin, C. (1981) *Conversational Organization: Interaction Between Speakers and Hearers*. New York: Academic Press.

Goodwin, C. (1986) 'Between and within: alternative and sequential treatments of continuers and assessments'. *Human Studies*, 9: 205-18.

Goodwin, C. (1987) 'Forgetfulness as an interactive resource'. *Social Psychology Quarterly*, 50 (2): 115-31.

Greatbatch, D. (1988) 'A turn-taking system for British news interviews.' *Language in Society*, 17: 401-30.

Greatbatch, D. (2006) 'Prescriptions and prescribing: coordinating talk- and text-based activities', in J. Heritage and D. Maynard (eds), *Practicing Medicine: Structure and Process in Primary Care Encounters*. Cambridge: Cambridge University Press. pp. 313-39.

Greatbatch, D. and Clark, T. (2003) 'Displaying group cohesiveness: humour and laughter in the public lectures of management gurus'. *Human Relations*, 56 (12): 1515-44.

Greatbatch, D. and Clark, T. (2005) *Management Speak: Why We Listen to What Management Gurus Tell Us*. London: Routledge.

Greatbatch, D. and Clark, T. (2010) 'The situated production of stories', in N. Llewllyn and J. Hindmarsh (eds), *Organisations, Interaction and Practice: Studies in Real Time Work and Organising*. Cambridge: Cambridge University Press. pp 96-118.

Greatbatch, D. and Dingwall, R. (1997) 'Argumentative talk in divorce mediation sessions'. *American Sociological Review*, 62 (1): 151-70.

Greatbatch, D., Hanlon, G., Goode, J., O'Cathain, A., Strangleman, T. and Luff, D. (2005) 'Telephone triage, expert systems and clinical expertise'. *Sociology of Health and Illness*, 27 (6): 802-30.

Greatbatch, D., Heath, C.C., Luff, P. and Campion, P. (1995) 'Conversation analysis: human-computer interaction and the general practice consultation', in A. Monk and N. Gilbert (eds), *Perspectives on Human-Computer Interaction*. London: Academic Press. pp. 199-222.

Haakana, M. (1999) 'Laughing matters. A conversation analytic study of laughter in doctor-patient interaction'. Unpublished doctorate thesis, Helsinki: The University of Helsinki.

Heath, C. (1986) *Body Movement and Speech in Medical Interaction*. Cambridge: Cambridge University Press.

Heath, C., Hindmarsh, J. and Luff, P. (2010) *Video in Qualitative Research: Analysing Social Interaction in Everyday Life*. London: Sage.

Hepburn, A. and Bolden, G.B. (2012) 'The conversation analytic approach to transcription', in J. Sidnall and T. Stivers, T. (eds), *The Handbook of Conversation Analysis*. Oxford: Blackwell Publishing. pp. 57-76.

Heritage, J. (1984) *Garfinkel and Ethnomethodology*. Cambridge: Polity Press.

Heritage, J. (1995) 'Conversation analysis: methodological aspects', in U.M. Quasthoff (ed.), *Aspects of Oral Communication*. Berlin: De Gruyter. pp. 391-418.

Heritage, J. (1997) 'Conversation analysis and institutional talk: analysing data', in D. Silverman (ed.), *Qualitative Research: Theory, Method and Practice*. London and Thousand Oaks, CA: Sage.

Heritage, J. (2001) ' 'Ethnosciences and their significance for conversation linguistics', in K. Brinker, G. Antos, W. Heinemann, and S.F. Sager (eds), *Linguistics of Text and Conversation: An International Handbook of Contemporary Research*. Berlin: De Gruyter. pp. 908-19.

Heritage, J. and Atkinson, J.M. (1984) 'Introduction', in J.M. Atkinson and J. Heritage (eds), *Structures of Social Action: Studies in Conversation Analysis*. Cambridge: Cambridge University Press. pp. 1-15.

Heritage, J. and Clayman, S.E. (2010) *Talk in Action: Interactions, Identities and Institutions*. Oxford: Wiley-Blackwell.

Heritage, J. and Greatbatch, D. (1986) 'Generating applause: a study of rhetoric and response at party political conferences'. *American Journal of Sociology*, 92: 110-57.

Heritage, J.C. and Greatbatch, D. (1991) 'On the institutional character of institutional talk: the case of news interviews', in D. Boden and D.H. Zimmerman (eds), *Talk and Social Structure*. Cambridge: Polity Press. pp. 93-137.

Hester, S. and Eglin, P. (1997) *Culture in Action. Studies in Membership Categorization Analysis*. Washington, DC: International Institute for Ethnomethodology and Conversation Analysis and University Press of America.

Hoey, E.M. and Kendrick, K.H. (2017) 'Conversation analysis', in A.M.B. de Groot and P. Hagoort (eds), *Research Methods in Psycholinguistics: A Practical Guide*. Oxford: Wiley-Blackwell. Available at: http://pubman.mpdl.mpg.de/pubman/item/escidoc:2328034/component/escidoc:2328033/CAmethods_RMP.pdf (last accessed 28 June 2017).

Holmes, J. and Marra M. (2006) 'Humor and leadership style'. *Humor – International Journal of Humor Research*, 19 (2): 119-38.

Holmes, J. and Stubbe, M. (2003) *Power and Politeness in the Workplace: A Sociolinguistic Analysis of Talk at Work*. London: Longman.

Huczynski, A. (1993) *Management Gurus: What Makes Them and How to Become One*. London: Routledge.

Hughes, J.A., O'Brien, J., Randall, D., Rouncefield, M. and Tolmie, P. (2001) 'Some "real" problems of "virtual" organisation'. *New Technology, Work and Employment*, 16: 49-64.

Huisman, M. (2001) 'Decision-making in meetings as talk-in-interaction'. *International Studies of Management and Organization*, 31 (3): 69-90.

Hutchby, I. and Wooffitt, R. (1998) *Conversation Analysis: Principles, Practices and Applications*. Cambridge: Polity Press.

Jackson, B.G. (1996) 'Re-engineering the sense of self: the manager and the management guru'. *Journal of Management Studies*, 33 (5): 571-90.

Jackson, B.G. (2001) *Management Gurus and Management Fashions*. London: Routledge.

Jarvenpaa, S.L. and Leidner, D.E. (1999) 'Communication and trust in global virtual teams'. *Organization Science*, 10: 791–815.

Jayyusi, L. (1984) *Categorization and the Moral Order*. Boston, MA: Routledge and Kegan Paul.

Jefferson, G. (1988) 'On the sequential organization of troubles-talk in ordinary conversation'. *Social Problems*, 35(4): 418-441.

Jefferson, G. (1989) 'Preliminary notes on a possible metric which provides for a "standard maximum" silences of approximately one second in conversation', in D. Roger and P. Bull (eds), *Conversation: An Interdisciplinary Perspective*. Clevedon: Multilingual Matters. pp.166–96.

Jefferson, G. (2004) 'Glossary of transcript symbols with an introduction'. In G.H. Lerner (ed.), *Conversation Analysis: Studies from the First Generation*. Amsterdam: John Benjamins. pp.13-31.

Jefferson, G., Sacks, H. and Schegloff, E.A. (1987) 'Notes on laughter in the pursuit of intimacy', in G. Button and J.R.E. Lee (eds), *Talk and Social Organisation*. Clevedon: Multilingual Matters. pp.152-205.

Kangasharju, H. and Nikko, T. (2009) 'Emotions in organizations: joint laughter in workplace meetings'. *Journal of Business Communication*, 46: 100-19.

Kania, N. and Gruber, T. (2013), 'Understanding satisfying service encounters in retail banking – a dyadic perspective'. *International Journal of Services, Economics and Management*, 5 (3): 222-55.

Kasper, G. and Wagner, J. (2014) 'Conversation analysis in applied linguistics'. *Annual Review of Applied Linguistics*, 34: 1-42.

Kikoski, J.F. (1998) 'Effective communication in the performance appraisal interview: face-to-face communication for public managers in the culturally diverse workplace'. *Public Personnel Management*, 27 (4): 491-513.

Kikoski, J.F. and Litterer. J.A. (1983) 'Effective communication in the performance appraisal interview'. *Public Personnel Management*, 12 (1): 33-42.

Kitzinger, C. and Frith, H. (1999) 'Just say no? The use of conversation analysis in developing a feminist perspective on sexual refusal'. *Discourse and Society*, 10, 293-316.

Knoblauch, H., Schnettler, B., Raab, J. and Soeffner, H. (2006) *Video Analysis – Methodology and Methods: Qualitative Audiovisual Data Analysis in Sociology*. Frankfurt: Peter Lang.

Larsson, M. and Lundholm, S.E. (2013) 'Talking work in a bank: a study of organizing properties of leadership in work interactions'. *Human Relations*, 66 (8): 1101-29.

Lerner G.H. (2004) 'Introductory remarks', in G.H. Lerner (ed.), *Conversation Analysis: Studies from the First Generation*. Amsterdam: John Benjamins, pp: 1-11.

Llewellyn, N. and Hindmarsh, J. (2013) 'The order problem: inference and interaction in interactive service work'. *Human Relations*, 66 (11): 1401-26.

Madlock, P.E. (2008) 'The link between leadership style, communication competence, and employee satisfaction'. *Journal of Business Communication*, 45: 61-78.

March, J. (1994) *Primer on Decision Making: How Decisions Happen*. New York: Simon & Schuster.

Markman, K.M. (2009) '"So what shall we talk about": openings and closings in chat-based virtual meetings'. *Journal of Business Communication*, 46 (1): 150-70.

Maynard, D.W. and Clayman, S.E. (1991) 'The diversity of ethnomethodology'. *Annual Review of Sociology*, 17: 385-418.

Maynard, D.W. and Clayman, S.E. (2003) 'Ethnomethodology and Conversation Analysis', in L. Reynolds and N. Herman-Kinney (eds), *Handbook of Symbolic Interactionism*. Walnut Creek, CA: Altamira Press. pp.173-202.

Mazeland, H. (2004) 'Responding to the double implication of telemarketers' opinion queries'. *Discourse Studies*, 6 (1): 95-115.

Mazeland, H. (2006) 'Conversation analysis', in K. Brown (ed.), *Encyclopedia of Language and Linguistics*. Oxford: Elsevier. pp.153-63.

Meyer, J.C. (2000) 'Humour as a double-edged sword: four functions of humor in communication'. *Communication Theory*, 10 (3): 310-31.

Mintzberg, H. and Waters, J. (1990) 'Does decision get in the way?' *Organization Studies*, 11 (1): 1-6.

Mullany, L. (2011) 'Gender, language and leadership in the workplace'. *Gender and Language*, 5 (2): 303-16.

Nielsen, M.F. (2009) 'Interpretative management in business meetings: understanding managers' interactional strategies through conversation analysis'. *Journal of Business Communication*, 46 (1): 23-56.

Oshima, S. (2014) 'Achieving consensus through professionalized head nods: the role of nodding in service encounters in Japan'. *Journal of Business Communication*, 51 (1): 31-57.

Pomerantz, A. (1975) 'Second assessments: a study of some features of agreements/disagreements'. Unpublished PhD thesis, University of California, Irvine.

Pomerantz, A. (1978) 'Compliment responses: notes on the cooperation of multiple constraints', in J.N. Schenkein (ed.), *Studies in the Organization of Conversational Interaction*. New York: Academic Press. pp.79-112.

Pomerantz, A. (1984) 'Agreeing and disagreeing with assessments: some features of preferred/dispreferred turn shapes', in J.M. Atkinson and J. Heritage (eds), *Structures of Social Action: Studies in Conversation Analysis*. Cambridge: Cambridge University Press. pp.57-101.

Pomerantz, A., and Denvir, P. (2007) 'Enacting the institutional role of chairperson in upper management meetings: the interactional realization of provisional authority', in F. Cooren (ed.), *Interacting and Organizing: Analyses of a Management Meeting*. Mahwah, NJ: Lawrence Erlbaum. pp. 31–51.

Pye, A. (2005) 'Leadership and organizing: sensemaking in action'. *Leadership*, 1 (1): 31–50.

Rost, J.C. (1991) *Leadership for the Twenty-first Century*. Westport, CO: Praeger.

Sacks, H. (1974a) 'An analysis of the course of a joke's telling in conversation', in J. Sherzer and R. Bauman (eds), *Explorations in the Ethnography of Speaking*. London: Cambridge University Press. pp. 337–53.

Sacks, H. (1974b) 'Some consideration of a story told in ordinary conversations'. *Poetics*, 15: 127–38.

Sacks, H. (1992) *Lectures on Conversation*, 2 volumes, edited by Gail Jefferson with an introduction by Emanuel A. Schegloff. Oxford: Basil Blackwell.

Sacks, H., Schegloff, E.A. and Jefferson, G. (1974) 'A simplest systematics for the organization of turn taking for conversation', *Language*, 50: 696–735.

Samra-Fredericks, D. (1998) 'Conversation analysis', in G. Symon and C. Cassell (eds), *Qualitative Methods and Analysis in Organisational Research*. London and Thousand Oaks, CA: Sage.

Samra-Fredericks, D. (2000) 'An analysis of the behavioural dynamics of corporate governance – a talk-based ethnography of a UK manufacturing "board-in-action"'. *Corporate Governance: An International Review*, 8 (4): 311–26.

Schegloff, E.A. (1968) 'Sequencing in conversational openings'. *American Anthropologist*, 70 (6): 1075–95.

Schegloff, E.A. (1972) 'Notes on a conversational practice: formulating place', in D.N. Sudnow (ed.), *Studies in Social Interaction*. New York: Free Press. pp. 75–119.

Schegloff, E.A. (1987a) 'Between macro and micro: contexts and other connections', in J. Alexander, B. Giesen, R. Munch and N.J. Smelser (eds), *The Micro–Macro Link*. Berkeley and Los Angeles: University of California Press. pp. 207–34.

Schegloff, E.A. (1987b) 'Some sources of misunderstanding in talk-in-interaction'. *Linguistics*, 25 (1): 201–18.

Schegloff, E.A. (1988) 'Goffman and the analysis of conversation', in P. Drew and T. Wootton (eds), *Erving Goffman: Exploring the Interaction Order*. Cambridge: Cambridge University Press. pp. 89–135.

Schegloff, E.A. (1991) 'Reflections on talk and social structure', in D. Boden and D.H. Zimmerman (eds), *Talk and Social Structure: Studies in Ethnomethodology and Conversation Analysis*. Cambridge: Polity Press. pp. 44–70.

Schegloff, E.A. (1992a) 'On talk and its institutional occasions', in P. Drew and J. Heritage (eds), *Talk at Work: Interaction in Institutional Settings*. Cambridge: Cambridge University Press. pp. 101–34.

Schegloff, E.A. (1992b) 'In another context', in A. Duranti and C. Goodwin (eds), *Rethinking Context: Language as an Interactive Phenomenon*. Cambridge: Cambridge University Press. pp. 193–227.

Schegloff, E.A. (1992c) 'Repair after next turn: the last structurally provided defense of intersubjectivity in conversation'. *American Journal of Sociology*, 97: 1295-345.

Schegloff, E.A. (1992d) 'Introduction', in *Harvey Sacks: Lectures on Conversation*, 2 volumes, edited by Gail Jefferson with an introduction by Emanuel A. Schegloff. Oxford: Basil Blackwell. pp. ix-lxii

Schegloff, E.A. (1995) 'Discourse as an interactional achievement III: the omnirelevance of action'. *Research in Language and Social Interaction*, 28: 185-211.

Schegloff, E.A. (1997) 'Whose text? Whose context?' *Discourse and Society*, 8: 165-87.

Schegloff, E.A. (1998) 'Reply to Wetherell'. *Discourse & Society*, 9 (3): 423-6.

Schegloff, E.A. (1999a) '"Schegloff's texts" as "Billig's data": a critical reply'. *Discourse and Society*, 10 (4): 558-72.

Schegloff, E.A. (1999b) 'Naivety vs. sophistication or discipline vs. self-indulgence: a rejoinder to Billig'. *Discourse and Society*, 10: 577-82.

Schegloff, E.A. (2007) *Sequence Organization in Interaction: Volume 1: A Primer in Conversation Analysis*. Cambridge: Cambridge University Press.

Schegloff, E.A. and Sacks, H. (1973) 'Opening up closings'. *Semiotica*, 7: 289-327.

Scheuer, J. (2014) 'Managing employees' talk about problems in work in performance appraisal interviews'. *Discourse Studies*, 16 (3): 407-29.

Schmitt, R. (2006) 'Interaction in work meetings', *Revue francaise de linguistique appliqué*, 11 (2): 69-84.

Schnurr, S. and Chan, A. (2011) 'Exploring another side of co-leadership: negotiating professional identities through face-work in disagreements'. *Language in Society*, 40 (2): 187-210.

Schwartzman, H.B. (1989) *The Meeting: Gatherings in Organizations and Communities*. New York: Springer US.

Searle, J.R. (1969) *Speech Acts*. Cambridge: Cambridge University Press.

Simon, H.A. (1976) *Administrative Behaviour: A Study of Decision-Making Processes in Administrative Organization*. Third edition. London: The Free Press, Macmillan Publishers.

Stevanovic, M. and Peräkylä, A. (2012) 'Deontic authority in interaction: the right to announce, propose, and decide'. *Research on Language and Social Interaction*, 45 (3): 297-321.

Stivers, T. (2013) 'Sequence organization', in J. Sidnell and T. Stivers (eds), *The Handbook of Conversation Analysis*. Chichester: Wiley-Blackwell. pp. 191-209.

Stivers, T., Enfield, N. J., Brown, P., Englert, C., Hayashi, M., Heinemann, T., Hoymann, G., Rossano, F., de Ruiter, J.P., Yoon, K-E. and Levinson, S.C. (2009) 'Universals and cultural variation in turn-taking in conversation'. *PNAS*, 106, 10587-92.

Sundland, E. (2004) 'Feeling by doing – the social organization of everyday emotions in academic talk-in-interaction'. Dissertation, Karlstad University Studies.

Svennevig, J. (2008) 'Exploring leadership conversations'. *Management Communication Quarterly*, 21: 529-36.

Svennevig J. (2012) 'Interaction in workplace meetings' (Special issue on interaction in workplace meetings) *Discourse Studies*, 14(1): 3-10.

Taylor, J.R. and Robichaud D. (2007) 'Management as metaconversation: the search for closure', in F. Cooren (ed.) *Interacting and Organizing*. Mahwah, NJ: Lawrence Erlbaum. pp.5-30.

Taylor, J.R. and Van Every, E.J. (2010) *The Situated Organization: Case Studies in the Pragmatics of Communication Research*. New York: Routledge.

ten Have, P. (1999) *Doing Conversation Analysis: A Practical Guide*. London: Sage.

ten Have, P. (2004) 'Methodological issues in conversation analysis'. Available at: www.paultenhave.nl/mica.htm (last accessed 12 June 2017).

ten Have, P. (2012) 'Conversation analysis and ethnomethodology'. *The Encyclopedia of Applied Linguistics*, doi: 10.1002/9781405198431.wbeal1337

Tsoukas, H. and Chia, R. (2002) 'On organizational becoming: rethinking organizational change'. *Organization Science*, 13 (5): 567-82.

Wasson, C. (2000) 'Caution and consensus in American business meetings'. *Pragmatics*, 10 (4): 457-82.

Weick, K.E. (1979) *The Social Psychology of Organizing*, 2nd edn. Reading: Addison-Wesley.

Weick, K.E. (1995) *Sensemaking in Organizations*. Thousand Oaks, CA: Sage.

Whalen, J., Zimmerman, D.H. and Whalen, M. (1988) 'When words fail: a single case analysis'. *Social Problems*, 35 (4): 335-62.

Wilson, T.P. and Zimmerman, D. (1986) 'The structure of silence between turns in two-party conversation'. *Discourse Processes*, 9: 375-90.

Wittgenstein, L. (1953) *Philosophical Investigations*. Oxford: Blackwell.

Yukl, G. (2002) *Leadership in Organizations*. Upper Saddle River, NJ: Prentice Hall.

INDEX

NOTE: Page numbers in *italic* type refer to tables.

Fold a Crab

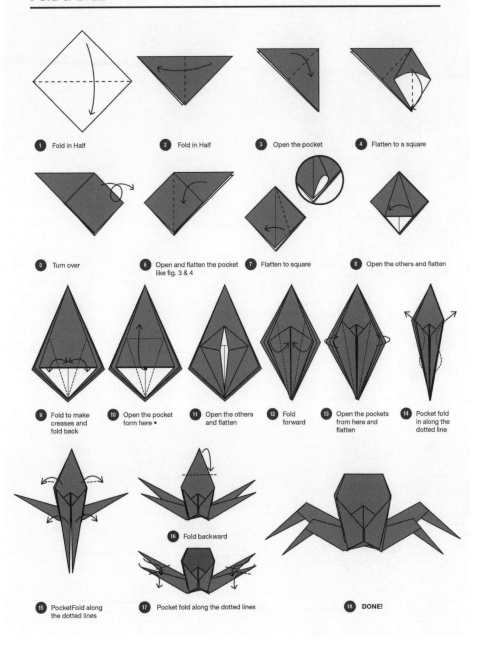

1. Fold in Half
2. Fold in Half
3. Open the pocket
4. Flatten to a square
5. Turn over
6. Open and flatten the pocket like fig. 3 & 4
7. Flatten to square
8. Open the others and flatten
9. Fold to make creases and fold back
10. Open the pocket form here •
11. Open the others and flatten
12. Fold forward
13. Open the pockets from here and flatten
14. Pocket fold in along the dotted line
15. PocketFold along the dotted lines
16. Fold backward
17. Pocket fold along the dotted lines
18. DONE!